T0144804

Supercharged Selling

Supercharged Selling

By Warren Greshes

MEDIA

Published 2018 by Gildan Media LLC
aka G&D Media
www.GandDmedia.com

FIRST EDITION 2018

Front Cover design by David Rheinhardt of Pyrographx

Interior design by Meghan Day Healey of Story Horse, LLC

Library of Congress Cataloging-in-Publication Data is available upon request

ISBN: 978-1-7225-0024-5

10   9   8   7   6   5   4   3   2   1

Contents

Foreword

Successful people do all the things that unsuccessful people are unwilling to do. You've got to be willing to do things that everybody is not willing to do. You've got to be willing to be different if you want to be successful in life, if you want to be successful in your careers. You've got to be willing to separate yourself from your competition. It all comes from within. It's your commitment to being the best. It's your attitude, thinking that what I do is terrific, what I do is great, what we have to sell is the best. If you don't believe in who you are and what you do, no one else will believe it and that's attitude, that's commitment.

Welcome to *Supercharged Selling.* In this book, Warren Greshes tells you how you can develop inner motivation to increase your sales performance and reduce your fear of failure and rejection. He shows you how small changes made on a regular basis can bring you big results, and he gives you the tools for setting goals, so you can make all your dreams a reality.

Warren Greshes is one of the most inspiring sales performance experts and motivational speakers I've ever known. As founder and president of SPEAKING OF SUCCESS, he knows what it takes to get ahead and he's ready to share with you the secrets that lead to a more meaningful and rewarding career.

—Bob Muesel

Introduction

There are three things I want you consider as you start to read this book. The first thing is something that many of you have achieved at some point in your lives and careers, but is also something that you strive for every single day, and that is **success**.

The second thing I want to talk about is something you must have in order to be successful and what that is **commitment.** I'm talking about a burning desire from within to do whatever it takes to be successful, to be great, to be the best, because I don't think you are reading this because you did not want to be successful, because you did not want to be great at who you are and what you do. I am sure you do not get up in the morning and say, "I just can't wait to be mediocre today."

The third and most important thing I want to talk about is you, and why are you here. I don't just mean sitting there reading this book. Why do you get up in the morning? What is your motivation? What is your sense of purpose? What drives you every single day? What makes you get up and say, "I want to go to work today?"

What it is that makes you move forward every single day with that very real and focused sense of purpose? What are your goals, what are you dreams, what are your plans?

By the time you finish reading this book, I want you to know what it is that motivates you because the truth is, I cannot motivate you. **Motivation** has to come from within.

Motivation

In order to be successful, you must be self-motivated. No one can motivate you except yourselves. I can't do it. Your boss can't do it. Your spouse can't do it. Your parents can't do it. Your teachers can't do it. Only *you* can motivate you. Even though I am a motivational speaker, I can't motivate you. Although I can do a fire and brimstone talk and have you swinging from the chandeliers, 24 hours later you're going to wake up and you're going to say, "What was that?" Because you see, at a motivational talk it's all about external motivation. And external motivation, well that's real short-term stuff.

What you really need to develop is internal motivation. In this book I want to give to you the tools and the techniques that will allow you to be better able to motivate yourselves, because what do you do on the days when no one's around to push you? This is especially true for those of you in sales, who are out there on your own every single day. The only one that's there to push you is you.

I always laugh when I hear sales managers say, "Well, I get my people going every day. I motivate them. I kick them in the behind. That gets them going every day," and I always ask them, "That's really good, but what happens on the days when you're not there to kick them?" Good question. Nothing.

You are wrong when you believe that motivation is kicking someone in the behind. That is not motivation; that is called movement. The problem with movement is that it stops; but internal motivation is what keeps us going every single day.

Let's think about the difference between internal and external motivation. A major difference between the two is that external motivation is for the short term while internal motivation is long lasting. In order to succeed salespeople must have that internal motivation.

Salespeople, for the most part, are the kind of people that go out. They're out there all day or most of the day without anybody watching them, without anybody looking to see what they're doing. So, it's very easy for salespeople who are not internally motivated to sit in the coffee shop all day. A salesperson, more so than most any other profession, has to be self-motivated in order to keep going all day without that supervision, without that little push that a lot of us get from people that we work with.

Internal motivation comes from developing for ourselves a sense of purpose, short-and long-term goals, and the plan that will get us to our goal. If we wake up every morning knowing that we will do X amount that we set out to do, and if we know doing that every single day will get us that much closer to our ultimate short-and long-term goals, then the motivation to get up and do it every day becomes incredible.

When we look at people throughout history who have been incredibly successful or have achieved at a high level, we find that their methods for being successful were pretty much the same. They all talk about how they set goals, visualized themselves as successful and had a plan.

Attitude

Internal motivation is what uniquely defines the successful sales pro, but there's also a factor of attitude to consider. In order to be part of a winning situation, you need to keep your attitude in check.

Most of us know somebody who is a very depressing person. That person I call the perpetual headache people. No matter when you talk to them they always have a headache or they can always top any illness you have? How do you feel after talking to that depressing person for 10-15 minutes? Depressed.

Now let's consider the other side of the coin. Most of us also know somebody who is a very positive, very enthusiastic person. How do you feel when you talk to that person? You feel good.

And when you're walking down the street, or into a store, or onto a train you are likely to enjoy bumping into that very positive, very enthusiastic person coming at you. You go out of your way to say hello. You wave at them. You make sure you get at least a few seconds to talk to that person.

People run from depressing people and they run toward people that make them feel good, even if it's a salesperson. There's this strange thinking that no one wants to see a salesperson, that the worst thing that can happen is that a salesperson coming to call. No. The worst thing that can happen is that a depressing salesperson is coming to call. However, if I am a buyer, and I see that salesperson who makes me feel good, my door swings open, because doesn't everybody want to feel good? Everybody wants to be part of a winning situation and to associate with a winner.

You might have noticed that when people recommend their doctor they always say their doctor is top in their field? Doesn't anybody go to the third guy? Everybody's doctor is the top person in their field, because everybody wants that feeling of associating with a winner.

People want to associate with winners. What is that one thing that's going to show whether we are the person that people run towards or run away from? There's one thing and one thing only. Our attitude. That's right. Attitude is the whole key. It is your attitude, the way you feel about yourself, the way you feel about what you do for a living, the way you feel about the company you work for, the way you feel about the products and services you sell. If you don't believe in who you are and what you do, well then no one else is going to believe in it. That is attitude.

The most frequent question I get from managers and business owners is this: How do I find good people? It's so hard to find good people. There's such a lack of good people out there. What do I look for? First and foremost, look for attitude. Look for that person who's willing to do whatever it takes to get the job done.

Don't worry so much about their knowledge; don't worry so much about their skills. You know why? Because you can teach them whatever they're going to need to know, but it's hard to teach attitude. That has to come from within. That has to be inside and it is hard for you to instill that in somebody.

You can take a person with all the knowledge and all the skills in the world, but if they have a bad attitude, they're not going to use the knowledge and they're not going to use the skills. However, if you take somebody with limited skills, limited knowledge, but with a great attitude, that person will do everything they can to acquire the skills and knowledge to get the job done.

The cheapest commodity in the world is general knowledge. What makes general knowledge, or any knowledge, valuable, is the ability to organize it and act upon it, and only those people with a great attitude will do that.

What will determine whether you are the person that people wave at and walk towards and whether you are the person that they always look to grab a few seconds with, or whether you're the person that when they see you coming they start looking for something in their briefcase? It's your attitude, the way you feel about yourself, the way you feel about your job, your company, and the products and services you sell. If you don't believe in who you are and what you do, you cannot expect anyone else to believe it. That is attitude.

Is It Me or Is It Them?

How can we recognize when our attitude is making our customers run away from us; that they're not just being difficult?

I'll be perfectly honest with you. I think it's hard to recognize when your attitude is making customers run away from you, simply because most people refuse to admit that it's them. I think you've got to start being honest with yourself. Sometimes we have to talk to the customer. You know, you lose a customer or if someone stops buying from you or someone is avoiding you, you literally have to be honest and say, "Why?" Ask them why. What is the problem? Why aren't we doing business anymore? I think that could help you start to look inward.

It can be hard to be honest with yourself; you might refuse to believe it. Often, you can recognize it very simply. If they stop buying from you, if they keep avoiding you, or if maybe they're buying from your company, but going around you.

And what about the customers that make *us* feel lousy? What we can do about this, especially when it's one of our big customers?

There are a couple of things we can do. First of all, we have to open up the lines of communication. One important thing everybody has to understand, including salespeople, is that not everyone is just like us. There are different personality types and they need to be communicated with in different ways. One of the first things to understand is who am I, what am I like, what do I like, and then, who is this customer, what are they like, how do they like to be sold?

The second level of communication is to ask: How do I perceive the customer, and how does the customer perceive me? I might perceive a difficult customer as, for example, a real bean counter. Yet, the bean counter is looking at me when I walk in the door and is thinking, oh, great, here comes Mr. Space Cadet. So, the communication is not matching. Now is the time to start to understand who each other are and to think about how each other wants to be approached. Then approach it that way.

Attitude is the driving force behind our success, and without a winning attitude we won't achieve to our greatest potential. Everybody has their own idea of a winning attitude, and I often find people addressing attitude as a "feel good" type of subject. I want people to feel good, but I am not simply talking about a feel good program.

The whole feel good thing is very short term, as in "everybody stand up, turn to the person next to you and give them a great big hug." That's fine and dandy, but the next morning everybody wakes up and they're back to square one since there was nothing long lasting about that experience. That is short term stuff.

When I talk about a winning attitude it is in relation to our goals, our plans, our senses of meaning and purpose. Attitude comes from going out there every single day, shooting at something that we really want, and knowing that every single day we are getting closer to it and have a chance of getting it. That raises our attitude level. We feel so good about what we're doing and about where we're going that we don't just feel good, we feel great, like we can conquer the world. Our goal is to raise that attitude level to the point where it is long lasting, steadfast and not just a short term "feel good" type of thing.

What to do when you're having a bad day, when you say, "I'm feeling lousy, I'm not going to be a success?"

There are some days like that. When you recognize you have a bad attitude, at first you might not want to get in front of people on a day like that.

But keep reading! What we are talking about cultivating a long view; to look more long term than short term. And when we start doing that we eliminate a lot of those lousy days, we eliminate a lot of those feeling down type of days. We start to realize that one bad day is only one bad day. For people who are very short term oriented, one bad day just seems to kill their whole week, or their whole month. As you become more long term oriented and more of a long term thinker, a long term goal setter, and a long term planner, you start to see it as one bad day; an isolated incident. And tomorrow is another day.

You Just Have to Ask

As a customer, or a potential customer, it just amazed me how few salespeople ever asked me to buy, or even asked if they could see me on an appointment. I get calls from salespeople all the time saying, "Well, here's my product. Are you interested in it?" And even if I say yes, they say, "Great, can I send you some information on it?" And I always answer, "Sure." If they had said, "Great, can I come over and see you next Tuesday at three?" I also would have said, "Sure." But they never bother to ask for the sale, or they never bother to ask for the appointment.

I came up with an idea for an exercise for a sales seminar that would illustrate the point that the biggest reason you're not getting appointments or closing sales is you're just not asking. As a salesperson with a garment center background, I found that you have to make intangible things tangible. The best thing you can do for a prospect or a customer is to help them touch and feel the merchandise. Now I am going to share with you the tangible way I found to illustrate this very fundamental idea.

If you don't ask you don't get. I do somewhere near 100 talks every year all over the world. And you know what? Everywhere I go, people give me money.

And how did I ask? At every seminar I said, "Take out a piece of paper, a pencil, a business card, and a dollar bill, and pass up the business cards and the dollar bills." This was a reasonable request at a reasonable time. This is important. If I said, "Give me a $100 bill" what would you say? Do you have one on you? Not likely. It's not a reasonable request at a reasonable time.

Hardly anybody ever says, "What's this for?" They just give it to me, all because I asked. I've used this exercise all over the US and the world, from the UK to Singapore with over 2500 attendees. And they give me their dollars, all because I asked.

It even went a little further in Milwaukee a few years ago. It was the second time I was speaking in front of this particular group. My problem was this; the people sitting on the left had all seen me speak before. The people on the right had never seen me in their lives. Now, the people on the left, they walked in, and before they even sat down they started whipping out dollar bills. Why? They knew me. They knew they were getting them back.

The problem was this, if you know anything about human nature you know that whenever a group of people sees someone else moving a little too quickly they always get a little leery. They always figure it's got to be a trick. And that's what was happening. The people on the right are sitting there and they're saying, "Hold it. They've seen this guy before. They're moving awfully fast with that money. This must be a trick."

So they stop. If half my audience stops, there goes the whole routine. I didn't know what to do. So, I walked up to the first person I saw, I looked this guy right in the eye, and I said, "Do you want in or out?" And he said, "I want in." I said, "Give me a 20." I got a $20 bill.

I went to the next person. "In or out?" He said, "In, in." I said, "Give me a 20." I got another $20 bill. I went to the next person, "In or out?" This guy looks me right in the eye and he said, "I'm out." I turned my back on him and I walked away. I said, "All right, forget it, pal, you're out." He said, "No, no, please hold it. I want in." I said, "Give me another 20." I got another $20 bill. In fact, I got $60 extra, and I had no idea what "in or out" meant either.

So we can see the big message you have to ask, because one of the single biggest reasons you don't get what you want out of life, one of the biggest reasons you don't get what you want out of other people, and you better believe the single biggest reason that salespeople do not close sales is because no one ever asks for a thing. They have what I call "great conversations." After a sales call call and you say, "How'd it go?" "Oh, what a nice guy. We were together for hours. We had a great conversation." "Did he buy anything?" "Well, I don't think he really needed anything." "No, he didn't. Do you know why he didn't need anything? Because no one asked.

Did you notice what I did when someone would not give me a bill? What did I do?

I ignored him, I just passed him by. I walked away. Think about it, did I need everybody's dollar bill to prove my point? No. Do you need to sell everyone you come in contact with to be successful? No. So, why stop when someone says no? Why do you stand there and argue when someone says no? Why do you get frustrated and give up when someone says no? Why don't you just move on? Your time is limited, and all the time you waste standing there arguing with somebody who is saying no is more time on a loss, when you just could have moved on and picked up all the yeses sitting there on the ground.

Why don't salespeople like to ask? They're afraid someone's going to say no. And they're right, someone is going to say no. Someone has to say no. In fact, in your career as salespeople you will hear the word "no" far more often than you hear the word "yes." But it doesn't matter how many people say no. It only matters how many say yes. And the only way you're going to get more people to say yes is to get more people to say no. In fact, if all you did tomorrow morning was wake up and say, "Today I am going to go out there and get as many people to say no to me as possible," can you imagine what might happen? Someone might ruin your day and say yes.

You have to ask and it has to be a reasonable request at a reasonable time.

Here is another exercise to help illustrate XXX-WHAT? Take a sheet of paper and write down these numbers: 1%, 3%, 5%, 9%, 14%, and 68%.

These numbers represent the results of a survey that was conducted a number of years ago by the Rockefeller Corporation out of Pittsburgh. They interviewed people around the country from 2,000 different service-oriented companies and asked one question: why customers stopped buying. We've all had customers who, for one reason or another, have stopped being customers.

They found that one percent of the customers stop buying because they die. Three percent stop buying because they move away. That happens. People retire, move to another part of the country, move to another part of the world. It happens. But it's only 3%.

Five percent of the customers stop buying because they form other business relationships. For instance, have you ever had somebody say to you, "Listen, I've really enjoyed dealing with you, but my son/daughter just went to work for your competition," You know what, that happens, but it's only 5%.

Nine percent of the customers that will stop buying from you do so for competitive reasons. This means price.

The Myth of Price

I want to take a step back here for a second, because I want to attack the myth of price. Price is not what makes people buy. Yes, price might get you a sale, but price doesn't make you a customer. And you're not trying to make sales; you're trying to develop customers, because a sale is a one shot deal. A customer is someone who buys over and over and over, and you do not make your business success in life on one shot deals. You become successful in sales on repeat business. And repeat business is not done on price.

If you're a price salesperson you will eventually be in trouble, because let me tell you something about price. Price is the single easiest thing for your competition to duplicate. It's the easiest thing. If they just want to slash their price they can do it. Now, if all you're selling is price, if you're going around telling people, "Listen, you should buy from us because we have the lowest price in town," what's going to happen the day that somebody beats your price? What's the benefit? There is none. You've told the customer the only reason to buy from us is because of our price.

Do you want to make a sale, or do you want to make a customer? And believe me, there's a difference. There's a big difference between a customer and a sale. A sale is a one shot deal. A customer is the one who buys over and over and over again.

And price is not what makes people buy over and over and over again. Price is good for one thing. Price is good for one thing. It is good for getting people to buy the first time. It is an incentive that gets people to try you out. But once they try you out, you'd better show them why; that you're good, that what you do has value, that what you do has quality, because that's the only reason they're going to come back.

Quality, service, convenience, and value; that's what people buy. And that's what makes people buy. That's not only what makes them buy. That's what makes them come back.

But wait a minute! You may ask, in today's market, everybody seems to be looking only at the bottom line. How do we avoid falling into the trap of low price selling and re-focus our customers' attention back on to quality, service, convenience, and value?

I'm not so sure that customers are only looking at the bottom line and using that context of "only looking for price." I think they really want quality, service, convenience, and value, but the reason that they're looking at price so much is because they're not getting quality, service, convenience, and value often enough, so that they're forced to buy price.

I think you have to sell the customer or the potential customer on what the product and service can do for them and how it can fill their needs, because if people get what they want and get what they need, they will pay for it because you've made their lives easier, and price will not be as big an object.

Look at Disneyland as an example. If you've ever visited one of these theme parks, you know it's an expensive proposition. But they work so hard on making your day, on making your visit a great experience, and by giving you so much extra value and making sure that everything about that day is perfect, it doesn't seem like a lot of money once you finish paying it.

Building Trust

Service is something that everybody stresses. How do you get around the perception that everyone only talks a good service game?

It's really difficult to make a new customer, or a potential customer, believe that you do more than talk a good game. If you want to be successful as a salesperson you have to build trust. And the only way to build trust is to prove it to them. And the only way to prove it to them is to first get the customer.

In other words, if I'm trying to sell you something and I tell you that we give the greatest service and that you should trust us, to tell you the truth, why should you? Why should I trust you, why should you trust me if we don't know each other and you've never dealt with me before? You have no reason to trust me.

The only way to prove that we do more than talk a good game is to take care of all their needs. And if they do have a problem, to alleviate that problem quickly and to alleviate it well, and to do it with the least amount of hassle possible.

Price as Strategy

When is it a good strategy to use lower price to make a sale?

Lower price as a strategy to make a sale could be useful if I was trying to penetrate a brand new market, trying to grab some market share, and trying to show people that I am good at what I do in this particular market, especially if I was an unknown in this market. I would never approach a new prospective customer in my own market where I already have a foothold and try to give them an incentive to buy by lowering the price right off the bat.

There are some very logical approaches to developing a new market by using price as an incentive. Let's think about how this can be done rather effectively.

Remember when Japanese cars first entered the US market? They were the cheapest cars. Are they the cheapest cars anymore? No, in many cases they're the most expensive cars. But what they did was they gave you the incentive to buy it, and then they gave you a car that wouldn't break down.

In order to capture market share, when they first introduced cars into this market, where they have never been before, they used price, at first. Why? To get people to try something for the first time, price is a good incentive. And once you to try our product we will service you until you have no choice but to keep using us, no matter what the price is.

One of the smartest companies I've seen is McDonald's. McDonald's understands so well what people want. Their corporate motto is Q, S, C, and V; Quality, Service, Convenience, and Value. Not once do they mention food. They don't say Quality, Service, Convenience, and Food. They don't say Quality, Service, Convenience, and Cheap. They say Quality, Service, Convenience, and Value, because that's what people want.

It doesn't matter what it costs. What matters is what you're getting for what it costs. You get what you pay for. There's an old Far Eastern saying, "When you pay peanuts you get monkeys." Think about McDonald's. Watch their commercial; food, folks, and fun. "Not tonight. You don't want to cook dinner. Come on down. Have a Big Mac tonight. Bring the whole family down. We will make your life easier."

They're amazing. They always seem to know what you want and when you want it. They're always looking to make it fun, to make it convenient. They keep it clean. They do all the things they know that people want. They make it easy for you to buy.

We all want our lives made easier when we're buying something. And when that experience is pleasant, we feel good about doing repeat business with that same salesperson. How do we go about creating a pleasant buying experience for our customers so that they will want to see us again?

Don't we always want to shop in the stores that make buying a pleasant experience? Don't we always want to go to the places that we know if we have a problem it's not going to be a problem? I think those are the kinds of things that customers want from salespeople. They just want everything to be easy. The salesperson who makes everything easy is the one who's always welcome in the customer's office.

This is about developing a personal relationship with the customer. People don't buy from companies, or from organizations. People buy from other people. The attitudes and the perceptions that customers will form of your company only comes from the people they deal with.

When a customer hears the name of a company that they buy from, they don't see in their mind the picture of a building. They see in their mind the picture of the salesperson's face, the person they deal with. Because when they have a problem they don't call the company, they call the salesperson, because people buy from people.

Service

What are some hints to persuade our customers that we're trying to make their lives easier?

Don't just call your customers when you want to sell them something. A lot of salespeople do that, they only seem to show up when they want an order, or when they want a sale. And believe me, customers start to feel that. They know, okay, here's this guy, he's calling again, and he probably wants me to buy something. The top sales-people keep in touch with their clients on a regular basis. Clients feel good about salespeople who call them up just to say hello, just to make sure everything's okay without any ulterior motive.

I think that is a critical point in showing people that I care. How else do you show somebody you care? You're always looking to make their lives easier and you're look-ing to establish relationships. You're not so much looking to close a sale. You're looking to establish a relationship which develops a customer.

One of the reasons people buy from salespeople is that they feel the sales rep really understands what they want. And one of the best examples of a company under-standing their customers' desires is McDonald's. They al-ways know what their customers want when they want it.

I travel a lot, and when you travel as much as I do you're always susceptible to poor eating habits. Now, I don't like fast food. I really try to stay away from those places. And I'm pretty good at it. But, if you were to ask me where do you eat when you do end up eating that sort of stuff? I will tell you 90% of the time I end up at McDonald's. Do you know why I end up at McDonalds 90% of the time?

Because McDonald's, for some reason, are always where you are, at the exact moment that you are hungry. How do they know? I'm convinced if I was in the Sahara Desert and I got hungry and I said, "Oh, lunchtime," all I'd have to do is turn around and there would be golden arches behind me.

I'll never forget a number of years ago when I first started speaking, I had done a morning speech in New Haven, Connecticut, and had to do an afternoon speech in South Jersey, about 140 miles away. I got in my car, on Interstate 95, and I just started flying down that highway. I'm starving. I haven't eaten all day. It's right around lunchtime. I didn't want food. I just wanted to eat. All I wanted to do was roll down the window, stick out my hand, and have someone go, whack, and go whoom like that, because I didn't have time to stop.

All of a sudden I see one of those signs, you know those trick food signs, the ones that say, "Food, Next Exit." You get off at the next exit, and what's at the bottom of the road? Nothing. Just an arrow that says "Food," and then you've got to drive another 15 miles in that direction.

Finally, you find the food. You've got to get out of your car, you've got to go inside, eat the food, get back in your car. And now you find you just can't cross the other side of the road because there's a divider. So you've got to go another 15 miles, come back another 30 miles, and you've wasted all this time. Did you ever drive in Jersey, right? You can't make a left in Jersey, right? If you miss your exit you've got to go to Pennsylvania and take a U-turn.

So, I said, "I'm not going to be fooled by a trick food sign anymore," so I kept going. I drive a little further down this highway and all of a sudden there it is: a billboard. It says "McDonald's." It doesn't say "Food." It doesn't say "Cheap." It says "Easy Access Off. Easy Access On." I said, man, how did they know I was coming?

They know what people want. They know that if you're flying down that highway you don't care about food. You want to eat. They know if you're flying down that highway you don't have the time to go driving 30 miles out of your way. You want to be able to get off that road, eat, and get right back on that road. So, what did they do? They put up a billboard that said, "Here, this is what you want. Come and get it." That's why they do business, folks. It's not price. It's not price that drives the buyer's engine. It's quality. It's service. It's convenience. It's value.

Wants Vs Needs

Let's get back to why customers stop buying; 14% of the customers that stop buying, stop buying because of product dissatisfaction. Now, what does that mean? Very simply, product dissatisfaction means that somebody bought something that he or she did not want or need. And you know whose fault that is? Yes, it's yours. When somebody buys something that he or she does not want or need, the first thing they figure out they don't want or need is you. The only way to develop long term, loyal customers is to find out what people want, find out what people need and give it to them. The problem is, most people don't buy what they need. Most people only want to buy what they want. The problem is, what they want is not what they really need. And if you only give them what they want, they finally figure out long term it's not what they needed. Now they don't want you. It's too late to come back and say, but that's what you wanted, because not a single buyer in this world will ever admit that the bad buy was their fault.

How many times have you ever been called in by a buyer who said to you, "Listen, I know this wasn't the right thing for me to buy. I shouldn't have made you sell this to me, and really it's all my fault so we're going to just keep doing business. From now on I'm just going to listen to everything you say." That would be never.

You do have to give them what they want, but you really have to give them what they need. The key to selling is to give people what they need disguised as what they want because if you don't give them what they need they don't come back.

You must start to look long term because that's what you want, long-term customers. Salespeople whose modus operandi is, I'm going to get in there; sell them whatever I can; get out of there as fast as I can are one-shot deal artists. They're not going to be successful.

When somebody wants to buy something that you know is the absolutely, positively wrong thing you've got to tell them. You've got to be prepared to turn down that sale. You know why? Because if you take that sale you lose the customer, if you turn down that sale you keep the customer.

What do you want? Do you want to keep the sale or do you want to keep the customer? You want to keep the customer. So, you've got to make sure they always buy what they need. And you know what? Just the act of turning down the sale is going to make them listen to you because no one's ever going to believe that a salesperson would turn down a sale.

I know that's hard to do, especially when you've got a manager telling you your sales are low, you've got to sell, you've got to sell, you've got to sell, but no, you don't have to sell; you have to develop customers. When you take a bad sale you lose a customer. You know as well as I do you want to keep the customer because the real money in sales is made on repeat business; not on one-shot deals.

No successful salesperson I've ever met has been successful on one-shot deals. You've got to be able to give people what they want and need. You got to put them both together.

I will turn down a sale before I will ever do a program or a speech that I know is wrong for that audience, because if I do the wrong speech I'm dead. I'll never work for that organization again, and they'll never refer me to anybody else. What did I gain? I got a one-time fee. Over the course of the next 20 years that one-time fee is not going to make a difference. Over the course of the next 20 years all that residual business I get from that client will. You have to give people what they need disguised as what they want.

The responsibility of the salesperson is to make sure the customer gets what he or she needs disguised as what he or she wants. But how do we determine the differences between the needs and wants of our customers? Isn't this all a matter of perception?

Yes and no. I think the wants are more a matter of perception. I think the needs are more a matter of what is real. The problem with most buyers is, they know what they want, but they don't necessarily know what they need. I think top salespeople know more what the customer needs.

My question to a salesperson, my question to any business owner is, do you know more about your industry, your product and your service than your customer knows? And of course the answer is yes, so it's up to you to try to understand their business, to try to understand their industry, to try to understand their company as much as possible. That will help you to uncover not just the short-term needs, but the long-term needs of the customer so that you can make sure that they get it by really understanding how they're going to use your product and service.

I'm a great believer in asking probing questions to discover the hidden agendas or requirements of the customer. One of the things I always talk about is, find out what answers you want to hear. That makes it easier to formulate the questions. And so you have to do a lot of pre-presentation planning; understanding what you want to say, understanding what you'd like to hear from the customer. That will tell you what kind of questions to ask.

The next thing you need to do naturally is to ask the right kinds of questions. Ask the kind of questions that will get you the answers that you need. And I think the question and probing part of the sales presentation is, without a doubt, the most critical part of the entire presentation because that is the part where you find out what the customer wants and needs.

And most important of all, you've got to learn how to listen. One of the things you can do in order to listen is when you're asking questions of the customer or the prospect, write down their answers. How do I know you're listening unless I see you writing?

You might be listening without writing, but I can only assume. If I see you writing down my answers I know for a fact you're listening, and if I see people are listening to me, you know what I do? I keep talking. So, if you want to get the customer to keep talking, write down the answers.

The interview process is really focusing on the customer and determining their needs so you can make the presentation that is totally focused on them. Selling is a matter of finding out what someone wants and needs, and making sure they get it all the time. That's it.

If your customer makes a bad buying decision, is there anything you can do to recoup from that situation?

First of all, how you recoup from a bad situation is try not to ever get into them. You really have to be strong enough to turn down the sale. You'll find that when you're willing to turn down a sale, the customer will be more willing to listen to you.

However, if you just can't get around it, if that customer insists on buying it and you know it's wrong; if it turns up bad, you're going to have to make good on it. If you really want to keep that customer you just have to make good on it and turn it around. Take it back or give them money back or make everything right on the next sale; that's the only way to do it.

The only way to do it is to just let them get everything back that they lost. I think you also have to point out, in a very diplomatic way, that this was their buying decision, and now, since I have alleviated your problem, and am going to live or die as the salesperson on your buying decisions, now can we please listen to what I have to say?

I've showed you that I'm willing to take responsibility and to make good if something goes wrong. Now what I want you to do is to listen to me. I think now they're going to be more willing to listen to you because they see you're willing to back it up.

Let's continue with why customers stop buying from us.

Here is the last one; 68% of the customers that will stop buying from you stop buying because of poor or indifferent attitude on the part of you or someone that works for or with you. Isn't that incredible; 68% of the customers you'll lose, you'll lose because of just poor attitude, poor service. Someone was nasty; someone didn't return a phone call; someone listened to a client's problem and said, "Oh, this guy is always complaining. Forget it, he's a nut." Someone took a complaint and swept it under the rug and didn't deal with it. Isn't that incredible?

Think about it. Think about it from your side as customers because every one of you is a customer. We're all consumers; we all buy things.

I want you to think about all the organizations, all the companies, all the stores that you stopped doing business with and why. It was usually because someone was nasty; someone didn't return a phone call; someone treated you as if you were just not important to their business. Did you ever call up a company with a complaint and you get customer service. You get somebody on the phone and you tell them your problem and they give you the line," Well, we can't really help you with that. This person who could is not here, so why don't you give us your name and number and we'll get back to you."

Have you ever had an occasion when they did get back to you? It does happen. Right? You pick up the phone and they're there, and what's your reaction? Shock. Now that's incredible. Think about that. What did they do? The minimum. They did what they were supposed to do. They did what they said they were going to do, yet you're shocked. Do you see how easy it is to beat your competition? Return a phone call, you beat your competition.

You see how we've come to not only expect poor service, but to accept poor service. We're conditioned. Do you ever see how you react when they return your phone call? They haven't done a thing, but you're so grateful that they did more than almost anybody else did, that even if they don't alleviate your problem you keep buying from them.

Think about it as a customer. Have you ever gone out to eat at a really fancy, nice restaurant?

You get all dressed up, go to one of these really nice places. The food's fantastic, the place is expensive, but the waiter or waitress was nasty. What did you do? Never went back, right? Did you tell anybody about the bad experience you had? Did you ever recommend anyone eat there? No, you never did. You never recommend any-one eat there. Food's great, you never tell anybody to eat there.

Now let's look at the other side of the coin. I want you to think about this place that you all know because you all know this place. You know the place you like, little neighborhood place; quick lunch, quick dinner on the weekend, maybe a couple quick drinks with friends.

Let's be perfectly honest about this, folks. The place is a bit of a dump the food, so-so. It's alright, but when you walk in the door they call you by your name. You know that place? What do you do? You go back.

Do you ever tell anybody about what a great place it is? Sure, you tell everybody. Do you ever bring other people with you? Sure, lots of other people.

Do you see what they did? They told you you were important; they told you they value and cherish your business, and you know how much it cost them to do that? Nothing. They remembered your name and bought your business for life.

The other place spent thousands on advertising, thousands on décor, thousands on a chef, thousands on everything, but they forgot to tell the help not to be nasty. The place you like; you know how much it cost them to decorate it? They probably won the furniture when they bought a full tank of gas. They probably microwave the food, yet they do what you want; they make you feel good.

They make it easy for you to buy. They make buy-ing a pleasurable experience, and you keep coming back.

You know what it is? It's attitude. That's all it is, that's what you buy; you buy attitude. The way you feel about yourself, the way you feel about your job, the products and service you sell. We all buy attitude. That's the whole ball of wax.

Customers buy attitude and that attitude puts us ahead of the competition. Is attitude the only competitive advantage that really lasts? Is it all that important?

I would answer that by saying no and yes. I say no because it's not the only competitive advantage that really lasts. There are other things involved. You have to have a quality product, you have to be a quality company. But, on the other hand, attitude is probably one of the most important things because we buy attitude. If you don't have a good attitude a lot of those other things are never going to matter.

Follow Up

What techniques promote a positive attitude towards us in the minds of our customers?

One thing that I feel is critical in promoting a positive attitude towards us in the minds of our customers it would be follow up. It never ceases to amaze me how many salespeople are just so awful at follow up. I think one thing that bugs me more than anything else is people that don't return their phone calls.

I'm not saying you have to return a phone call within five minutes; absolutely not. But, if you get back to people within 24 hours they're really pleased about that. I'm a bug about follow up. I'm constantly in contact with people, I return my phone calls always within 24 hours. I never just sell and disappear.

I think one of the things that is so critical is that ability to follow up. I'm just amazed at how many people approach me about trying to sell me something, get me interested in what they have to sell and then never follow up to find out if I want to buy. Now, my feeling is, if you're not even interested enough to take my money, what's going to happen if I actually do buy from you once you have my money?

Even though we have a winning attitude, some of our coworkers who deal with our customers may not. What can we do about their poor attitudes?

One of the problems with how our coworkers treat our customers stems from how our coworkers are treated. If someone works for you, if you're a manager, that person working for you is your customer. And how they treat the customer is really dependent on how they're treated. And if you expect your coworkers to service your customers the way you want them to be serviced then you have to service your coworkers. I think that is so critical.

We always want to fill the needs of our customers because we figure, if we fill the needs of our customers they become long-term, loyal customers. Well, doesn't it hold true, then, that if we fill the needs of our coworkers they become long-term, loyal coworkers? I think the key is to treat your coworkers the way you want them to treat your customers.

We've all experienced, from time to time, problems with our customers. Aren't these situations great opportunities for us to demonstrate the quality of our service, as well as our ability to take care of our customers?

Something going wrong is your opportunity. You may say, "If something goes wrong, we'll take care of you." How are you going to prove it unless something does go wrong?

You should encourage your customers to complain because by encouraging them to complain, that's the only way you're going to have an opportunity to fix it. When people have a complaint and they don't express it, usually what they do is they just walk away from the situation, and you lose the customer. I think when something goes wrong that's your opportunity to shine, that's your opportunity to back up what you said. I think the best example that I could ever find of this is Lexus.

When the Lexus first came out everybody hailed it as the most incredible car. Every magazine, every consumer report said, this was just an incredible driving machine. Yet, when the Lexus first came out it was recalled.

Opportunity or problem? Usually when a car gets recalled you get a letter from the automobile company saying your car's been recalled and to call your dealer. Now you have to go through the motions of calling your dealer hoping you can get an appointment. Then you've got to bring your car down, wait around to get it fixed, or you have to go back home, come back again, pick it up. Everything is a big hassle.

What did Lexus do? Lexus saw this as an opportunity. They called every single person that had bought this car; called them on the phone. They said, your car is being recalled. They told them what was wrong with it. They said, but don't worry, stay where you are. We're going to come to your front door, we're going to bring another car with us; we're going to take your car, leave another car for you to use in the interim. We're going to bring your car to the dealer; we're going to fix it. When that car is done being fixed we're going to bring it back to your house, take back the loaner car; no muss, no fuss, it's like nothing happened.

Now, if you owned a Lexus after that whole process ended would you be going around talking about the fact that your car was recalled? Of course not. You'd be going around talking about the fact of how they handled the recall. Because of the way they handled the recall and publicized it, their sales skyrocketed. They did the one thing everybody wants to know; what's going to happen should something go wrong?

What do you think is one of the biggest mistakes a company can do in the treatment of their customers?

One of the biggest mistakes that companies can make is to make it easier for them as the company than make it easier for us as the customers. It never ceases to amaze me how companies put in systems that make their life easier but puts the onus on the customer.

Here's an example that happened to me. My wife and I went to a local bar/restaurant because we wanted to see a friend of ours who was singing there. There was a whole group of people sitting at the table with us; some of them we knew, some of them we didn't know, some of them came for dinner, some of us had come just to have a few drinks. My wife and I had three drinks between us, and I turned to the waiter and asked, "Could you just give me a separate check for our drinks?" He looked at me, he said, "Oh, we can't do that. You see, this is all computerized and so your table gets one check."

"Oh, that's great." In other words, they bought this computer system so that the restaurant could make it easier for them, but harder on me as the customer. I now have to sit and figure out what that check says. They keep better tabs on everything for themselves, and make it totally difficult for the customer.

Do you have an example of what a company should do to make it a pleasant buying experience for a customer?

It's always been my feeling that if you want to make pleasant buying experiences for your customers first you sit down and say, what are some of the things customers dislike about dealing with companies such as ours, or industries such as ours, and then find a way to eliminate those dislikes?

I'll give you a great example. My wife and I were recently in Orlando for a convention, and we took one day and visited Epcot Center. What impressed me so much about that place was how they keep the lines moving. Everybody always talks about how the lines were so long; you had to wait forever.

Yes, the lines there were long. And in reality, it didn't take any less time to get from the back of the line to the front of the line than it takes in most other places, but what they do is, they snake the lines so that you're constantly moving. They understood one thing in the Disney Corporation; that one of the most unpleasant experiences you can have is to not just stand in line but to stand in one spot, because when you stand in one spot you get antsy, you get frustrated and you start to complain and you start to hate the experience. By snaking the line, they keep you moving.

While you might not be getting to the front of the line any faster, you're moving, so you have that sense of making progress, and standing in line doesn't become a chore. I just found it amazing that they made the whole standing in line thing a much less unpleasant experience. Why don't other places do that? Why don't they use snaked lines instead of just one long line?

And, basically, you know what the answer is? They don't care enough. And right away when you see something like those snaked lines you think, they cared enough to actually think of this. They cared enough to make an unpleasant experience just a little more pleasant, and because of that you want to keep going back there.

If we want to be outstanding salespeople we must have a winning attitude and a powerful desire to make our customer's lives easier. We need to be committed to doing the best for our customers in order to keep them coming back for the long term.

It's all attitude. It all comes from within. It's your commitment to being the best. It's your attitude that what

I do is terrific, that what I do is great, that what we have to sell is the best. If you don't believe in who you are and what you do no one else will believe it, and that's attitude; that's commitment.

Developing Attitude

We've talked about attitude. We've talked about commitments. But, where does it come from? Where does this attitude and commitment come from? What can we do to develop this kind of attitude and commitments in our own lives and our own careers?

You're not necessarily born with a burning desire to be the best or with a great attitude. Yet you can still develop them. I know. I did not have them. I was not a driven person. I was not a motivated person. I was one of those people just shuffling along in life, basically spinning my wheels every single day.

One of the things I speak about more often than anything else is the subject of commitment. When I first started speaking about commitment I started to wonder where does it all come from. What can we do to develop commitment? Where did I get this from?

The key is to answering this kind of question is to look back at your own life and your own experiences and your own turning points because we all have them. We don't think we have them. We always minimize our own experiences and our own turning points in our lives. But, when we look back we find out that they're there and so that's what I did.

I looked back at my life. I looked at what drives me every day and all of a sudden it hit me. It all came back to a set of questions that were asked of me almost 20 years ago. Unfortunately, for me, the true meaning of those questions did not sink in until almost 11 years later. But when it did it changed the entire direction of my life. When I look at, talk to, and read about all the successful people in this world they seem to have the ability to answer that set of questions that was asked of me almost 20 years ago. So let me go back 20 years.

Twenty years ago I graduated from college. Like so many other young people who graduate from college I had no clue; none, zip, zero. In fact, if I was one-quarter as smart as I thought I was I would've been real smart. I had no idea what I wanted to do with my life. I had no idea what I wanted to do with my career. I had spent four years majoring in snack bar.

You grow up your whole life and everybody tells you, you've got to go to college. Why? Well, you've got to go. Why? You've got to. All right. I'm going. Then they tell you, remember, you can never take that away from you when you've got that four-year degree. Doors will just swing open.

Now I'm standing there with my four-year degree. I'm waiting. Come on. Start swinging. Nothing's happening. So what did I do? I accepted an executive position at the local carwash. They made me the head wiper. That's what I did. I spent about four months working in this carwash after I graduated from college, saved up all the money I could, and four months later I put a pack on my back and I left for Europe like so many other young people back then.

The thing I love about traveling through Europe is that you can move from country to country with the same ease that here, we move from state to state, because the countries are so small. The only difference being that when you go from country to country you must pass through customs. The story takes place was on a train going from Paris, France to Munich, West Germany.

I'm on a train when all of a sudden the train stops. It's early in the morning, about 5 a.m. I wake up when the train stops, real groggy. I lift open the window shade and it's a dark, dreary, drizzly, foggy day and we're on the West German border. As a look out through the fog and the mist the only thing I could see is this group of West German border guards. Remember this is my first time ever outside the United States. I'm all by myself, not quite 21. It's early in the morning and I started to play up all these mental scenarios of things that really are not going to happen. All those old World War II movies that I grew up watching, where the border guards come on the train and ask to see your papers. They always ask for papers and then they drag you off the train. They beat you up. They throw you by the side of the road. Never to be heard from again.

I knew I had nothing to worry about. I had done nothing wrong, but I couldn't help being a little paranoid in the situation. The border guards came on the train. They started to grab passports and ask questions. And, finally they came to me and grabbed my passport. They looked at my passport and they looked at me. Again, and then again, they looked at my passport and they looked at me. And then finally they asked me those question; the questions that every single successful person can answer.

The true meaning of those questions did not sink in until almost 11 years later, and when it did it changed the entire direction of my life. Where have you been? Why are you here? Where are you going?

Unless you can answer those questions, unless you have a clear idea of where it is you want to end up and how you're going to get there, there's no way you can develop that sense of commitment or that burning desire to do whatever it takes to the be the best. The key to success and the key to achievement is to have a sense of purpose and a goal which gives us a reason to be committed to our own success.

Where have I been? Why am I here? Where am I going? These seem like logical questions to be asking yourself. But most people seem to have difficulty answering the first two questions and the last one stops them dead in their tracks. Why do you think it's so difficult to answer these questions?

I think we make it difficult to answer. One of the things we do to make these questions difficult to answer is to try to do it in our heads. Everybody tries to do this in their heads. You can't organize things in your head. You can't organize your life in your head. You can't organize anything in your head.

One of the keys to answering these questions is to get everything down on paper. Write down everything no matter what it is; just let it pour out of you. No matter what it is, whether you want it or not. Just get it all out of your head. Then once you've gotten everything down on paper then start to organize it and answer those questions.

Can you develop a sense of purpose without answering these three questions?

You cannot develop a sense of purpose unless you know where you want to end up. Part of your sense of purpose has to do with your destination. If you don't know where you want to end up you have no purpose, no vision.

Developing a Plan

How do you use these three questions as a basis for your sales plan?

Of course, you could use this as a basis for your sales plan. These three questions are the basis for your life. If they're the basis for planning your life they're obviously the basis for planning your sales. Let's analyze it. Where do you want to end up? That could be the basis for a sales plan.

What is your plan for this customer? You have a customer you want to start to sell. You have a customer you want to develop. Where do you want to end up with your customer? Where do you see yourself with this customer? Do you want to be their number one vendor? Do you want to be their number two vendor? Do you want to own 20% of their business? Do you want to own 50% of their business?

Where are you now with that customer? Are you at zero? Are you at 10%? Let's say I own 10% of that customer's business. I own 10% of the market, so to speak. I want to end up owning 50% of the market. That's where I want to end up.

Where am I going? I want to go to 50% of the market. I'm at 10%. That's where I am now. Where was I? A year ago I was at 2%. Now, today, where am I? I'm at 10%. I want to be at 50%. Now, once I've figured out those three questions, where have I been, where am I now, where am I going; now I can figure out a way to get there.

Without goals I have no direction in my life or career. Let's discover why people don't have their goals written down.

Do you know what I find incredibly scary? The fact that only 5% of all the people out there actually have goals. Do you know what's even scarier? Only 1% ever writes them down. Do you know the single biggest reason that people do not get what they want out of life? The single biggest reason don't get what they want out of life is because they never bother to figure out what it is.

If you don't know what you want how are you going to get it? And, if you don't know how you get it how are you going to get it? And, if you don't know what you want how do you know you didn't already have it but because you couldn't recognize what it was you just kind of let it pass you by? Now you laugh, but how many people do we know that have passed up all the greatest opportunities in their lives because at the moment that it was an opportunity they didn't recognize the opportunity because they didn't know what they were looking for and they just let it pass them by and when it was too late they recognized that that was what they wanted out of their lives and it was gone.

Ask most people what they want out of their lives and they talk in vagaries. They say things like, "Well, I want to make a lot of money." That's good. What's a lot of money? Or they'll say, "Oh, I want a better job." Better than what? Better than what I have. How much better? A little bit? A lot? Less than a bit? I want a bigger house. I want a nicer car. I want more. I want a lot. What does that mean? What's a lot of money? Think about it.

Let me ask you a question. How many sales do you have to make in order to make a lot? You probably answered, a lot. And next question: How many people do you have to present to to close a lot of sales to make a lot of money? A lot more than a lot. But now, how many appointments do you have to set up to get to present to a lot of people, to close a lot of sales, to make a lot of money? A heck of a lot. So now, how many people must you call to make a lot of appointments to get to present to a lot of people, to close a lot of sales, to make a lot of money?

How do you know when to stop? You don't? Yet you all stop every day. What are you doing right now? You're stopped. We stop every single day. And if you don't know what a lot is how do you know you didn't stop short?

Have you ever had one of those days where the first three people you call say, "Drop dead," and you might say, okay, that's a lot. How do you know you didn't have to speak to five people that day because you don't know what a lot is? Salespeople ask you that question all the time.

What's a Lot of Money?

I hear that question all the time and in response, I hear these vague answers, as if they're taking the numbers right out of the air.

It's not a matter of what the number is. It's a matter of what it's going to do for you because you understand something about money. Money is a vehicle; that's all it is. Money is a vehicle that allows you to live the type of lifestyle that you want to live. So, what do you really need to know? The type of lifestyle you want to live, what you want your life to look like. Once you've defined that, you will know how much money you need to support it.

If you don't know what you're going to do with the money what's the motivation to get it? There isn't any because money is not a motivator. No one ever gets up in the morning and says, "I just can't wait to get to work today because they pay me well." No one ever says that.

People do say things like, I really hate this job. I want to get a better job. I can't stand this place. I'd love to get out of here, but you know what? This is all I know. What else can I do? And besides, they pay me pretty well so I might as well stay. Whoa, talk about commitments. They pay me pretty well so I might as well stay.

Remember that job that you hated? Did you ever have an occasion to get a raise on that job? The day after you got the raise you came to work the next day. Did you still hate the job? You still hated the job just as much if not more.

The day after the raise the money meant nothing. It didn't make you any happier. It didn't make you any more productive. Money is not the motivator. What the money can do for us is what motivates us.

What's a lot of money? Single guys usually say a million dollars. For some reason single guys always say a million dollars. When I ask what they're going to do with it, they always say the same thing; they're going to buy a Porsche.

So now I ask, "do you need a million dollars to buy a Porsche?" "No." "Well, what do you need?" "Well, you need like $50,000/$60,000." "Do you really?" If you really wanted a Porsche couldn't you just lease it? What do you need for a lease? Nothing. So, "Do you have nothing today?" "Oh, yes." "Then, how come you don't have a Porsche?" Maybe it's not what they really wanted.

We must understand something about 'a lot.' Everybody's 'a lot' is different. What's a lot to you is not a lot to me or to him or to her. It does not really matter what your 'a lot' is. It only matters that you know what it is, because unless you know what it is, how are you going to formulate a plan to get it?

And remember, it's only 'a lot' if it's going to get you what you want, and, if you don't know what that is, how do you know you don't already have it and because you couldn't recognize it you just let it pass you by.

What do successful salespeople use for motivation?

Successful salespeople use everything else for motivation rather than money. It's not money itself; it is what the money can do for them. For most, it's about achieving a specific lifestyle or a certain position in their company. They have that competitive nature. They want to be the top person, the top producer.

What further motivates a lot of salespeople is that willingness to make a positive impact on their customers, on the people they deal with. The willingness to help the people they're selling to rather than just sell them. Those attitudes are what help successful salespeople make a lot of money.

Setting Goals

What's the difference between a goals oriented person and one that hasn't set any goals at all? Simply put, the difference is success or failure.

Is knowing what you want the same thing as having goals?

Knowing what you want is good. You have to know what you want in order to set the goal. How do we recognize an opportunity unless we first decide in our minds and on paper what that opportunity looks like? That's why people miss all the opportunities in their lives because when they appear, up they didn't recognize it was an opportunity and it passes them by. They finally figured out it was an opportunity after it was gone.

The world is filled with people who have war stories on all the great things they could've done with their lives if only they were smart enough to take advantage of the opportunity the second it hit. Well, they were smart enough; they just didn't bother to figure out what that opportunity was going to look like. And, you know what's even more amazing about those people? So many times they actually get what they wanted out of life but because they've never bothered to figure out what it is and because they've never been able to describe what it is they just kind of let it pass them by because they don't recognize it as the opportunity they've been waiting for their entire lives.

I come in contact so many people who just really truly believe that they're never going to get what they want out of life. They just really believe that, oh, I could never hope to be like that. I could never hope to be that rich. I could never hope to have that kind of a life.

Do you ever hear this? The only way I'm ever going to get something like that is if I win the lottery. I hate that. I hate lotteries. Well, I hate them and I love them. I hate them because I think they're nothing more than an education tax on people that can't afford it. But I love them because I never enter them so everybody else is paying my education tax for me. I think it's incredible how we've conditioned people to believe that the lottery is something they should be shooting for. It's incredible because you are not going to win. I don't know about Illinois, but the odds in New York State are 12 million to 1. You are not going to win. But there are people that bank their whole dreams on it.

I'll never forget a few years ago the top prize in New York State was $20 million and people were in line all around the streets for tickets. The media love this stuff and they always ask the same question, "What are you going to do with the money?"

One woman said, "I'm going to travel around the world." Another woman said, "I'm going to buy my mother a house." Some guy said, "I'm going to pay off my debts." As I'm watching this, I'm asking what kind of debt could this guy have? Could you imagine his Master-Card bill? Hold it, lady; do you need $20 million to travel around the world? Is your mother's house really going to cost $20 million? What's going to happen when you don't win because you're not going to win?

I wondered about the day after those numbers are called and what's going to happen to these three people? Is this woman never going to travel around the world? Is that other woman never going to buy her mother a house? Is this guy never going to pay off his debts? When they don't win are they just going to give up their life's dreams? Could it be true that all of their dreams are contingent on a 12 million to 1 shot? Is this what we've come to?

And they always ask, "Will you quit your job," as if the absolute best thing you could do is to stop working? What defines us more than our work? When we first meet each other don't we always ask "What do you do?"

A few months after that $20 million prize there was a $26 million prize, which was won by a Nigerian exchange student. He was on TV with lights all around; they're interviewing him and everyone is saying, boy, this is great. And it was. I was happy for him. He won $26 million. It is great. There's nothing wrong with it.

But do you know what he said? They asked him his feelings he said, "This is great. This can only happen in America." I heard that and I thought, think about that. Think about what he said.

I always thought the American dream was something very different. I thought it was that you could come here, you could do whatever you want and work as hard as you want. If you tried as hard as you could, you could make anything you wanted out of your life. The American dream still brings people here from all over the world.

Do you see what we're changing the dream to? Are we really telling people the best thing that could ever happen is to win the lottery? All I could think of was a group of immigrants in some foreign country sitting around a table, saying things like, if we pick numbers 3, 18, 26, 42, 48, 54. We go to America. We spent a buck and win and we get out of there. Is that something to be proud of?

We do seem to see our values changing. Everyone wants instant gratification, instant success, but success isn't winning a $26 million lottery. That's luck. If we wait for luck to do it for us we'll be waiting for a long time. We must attain our dreams on our own terms. But what about all those wonderful one-shot ideas or closing techniques that people talk about that are going to make them millionaires tomorrow?

Very simply, it's because your chances of becoming a millionaire tomorrow are so slim, those are often the examples brought up to salespeople. They always hear about that salesperson that closed that one big deal that put them over the top. They always hear about someone that made it big and it always sounds like the overnight success story.

To be perfectly honest with you, there's no such thing as an overnight success. In fact, a very successful speaker I know claims that it took her 15 years to become an overnight success. You hear those stories of the person who closed the big deal, but they never talk about all the chasing they did and all the years it took them to finally get to that big deal. And 99% of all salespeople would be better off if they just looked to constantly close deals no matter how big or how small, than chase that one big deal that, for the most part, they're either not going to get or it's going to take them off the track from consistent business.

In order to close deals and do a consistent amount of business, don't we need to quantify our sales goals just as we do our personal goals?

It is positive and necessary to know what we want in sales, just as it is to know what we want in our personal lives. You want to close the sale, yes, but I think more important than closing the sale is to close the right kind of sale. What do I mean by the right kind of sale? The right kind of sale is about what this customer is going to buy from me today, that's going to make him or her so happy with our product and our service that they're going to want to keep buying from us tomorrow and the next day and the day after that. In order to do that you have to formulate sales goals and sales plans just as you do in your personal life.

If we're waiting for something wonderful to happen to us we're going to be waiting a long time. We need to decide what our sales goals are and be willing to work hard to achieve them. There are many millionaires out there who can tell us that it can be done if we're willing to do the foot work.

In a survey publicized in *US News & World Report* a few years ago they found in the United States there were one million households whose net worth was a million dollars or more. That's one million millionaires. One million households means one out of every 100 households in this country has a net worth of a million or more. And, over 75% of those millionaires were self-made. And what's the really important news? There were twice as many millionaires whose jobs were in sales and marketing as there were doctors. Think about that. They surveyed these self-made millionaires further to find what their secrets were and discovered: sense of purpose, goals, plans, a commitment to excellence, efforts, hard work, smart work. In other words: if you know what you want, and you have a commitment to going out there and getting it, and working hard to get it, you've got a 1 in 100 chance. Not bad.

On the other hand, the state of New York will tell you all you need is a dollar and a dream and you've got a 12 million to 1 chance. So I ask you: 100 to 1 or 12 million to 1? The choice is up to you. The state of New York says, all you need is a dollar and a dream. Warren Greshes says, keep your buck, save it, and invest it in your future because all you really need is a dream.

How do we define success? What are some of the things we should be looking at and going after? Is everything just based on money? Are all our goals monetary goals? No; absolutely not.

I want to talk to you about the true definition of success, about other things besides money. The true definition of success means you are able to create a balance in your life. You must be able to reach a high level of happiness in more than one area in order to be truly successful, because, as we know, it's not all just about money.

The Five Levels of a Happy Life

If you want to tell me that success is simply equated with money, and that the successful people are the ones with the most money, then I will say that you consider drug dealers successful. Don't they have a lot of money? If that is the case, then they are the successes in the world. But, I don't think you really believe that, because you see in order to be truly successful you must reach a high level of happiness in a number of different areas. You must create that balance in your life. We have learned that the really successful people are those who have found that balance; who have found that lifestyle; who are happy in a number of different levels.

Before I start talking about creating happiness in the five areas of concentration you need for a successful life, I want to state loud and clear: They're all equally important; there is no one area more important than the other. Why don't we start talking about them now?

Financial Happiness

The first area of concentration where you need to achieve a high level of happiness is what I call financial happiness. What is financial happiness? Does that mean you make a lot of money? Not necessarily. Financial happiness means is that you earn the amount of money you need to support the lifestyle you want to live. So, what we really need to know is what the lifestyle we want to live is. That will tell us the amount of money we need.

Remember, everybody's 'a lot' is not the same. Not everybody has the same kind of lifestyle. Some people live a modest lifestyle and they choose to live a modest lifestyle. Some people live a lavish lifestyle, and they choose to live a lavish lifestyle. There are people who enjoy going camping for vacation. Other people enjoy going to four star hotels. What's the difference? It's what you enjoy; not what somebody else enjoys. That's what will determine whether you have reached financial happiness or not.

I'm talking about the people who really, truly don't need a lot of money to live. I know someone like that; one of the happiest people I know. He's a garbage man for the city of New York. In fact, if you ask him what he does for a living, he tells you he's a doctor of garbology. He is the happiest guy I know. He really is. When you ask him how he's doing, he says, "Fantastic" and really means it.

I've never met somebody that can make collecting garbage sound so exciting. He loves doing it. He loves his lifestyle. He makes the amount of money he needs to support his family in the way he wants to and the way they want to live. They do the things they want; they do the things they like.

I've never heard somebody talk about it like that. He says, "Oh, I love collecting garbage." I say, "Why?" He says, "Well, I like working outdoors." I had never equated it; to me working outdoors is being a forest ranger; not a garbage man. So what am I to say? Who am I? He's doing what he wants to do. He's living the lifestyle he wants to live, and he's making the amount of money he needs to live that lifestyle. That's true financial happiness. It doesn't matter what your 'a lot' is; it only matters that *you* know what it is.

Financial happiness is based on being able to live the lifestyle we want, but many of us define success by how much money we make. But, to equate success with money is insane.

Certainly, we need money. Let's face it. We live in society. We have to have a certain amount of money. We have to pay our bills; we have to be able to support a family. If we have children we want to be able to send them to college. We want to provide for our family no matter who we are and what we do. But, to equate success with money is insane.

Most sales reps measure sales success by the number of sales they close.
What criteria would you use to measure sales success? The criteria I use to measure sales success is are you, as

the salesperson, reaching your goals? In other words, is your production giving you what you want? I'll give you a good example of that. In the life insurance industry, most companies will tell an agent we want two applications a week, or two sales a week. You give us two sales a week and we're real happy.

And, the average life insurance agent works towards that goal, but what are they working towards? They're working towards the company's goal. My question to them is: What about you? It's all well and good to be satisfying the company. If the company's satisfied and you're not, you lose.

What is *your* goal? What is your goal, the one that would give you what you need to support the life you want to live? If you really needed five sales a week, but doing two sales a week, who are you satisfying? You're satisfying the company, but not yourself, and eventually you're going to drop out and everybody is going to lose. However, if you're satisfying your goal, which is five sales a week, then not only are you winning, but the company is winning even more. Everybody is winning, and as we all know, a win/win situation is the best situation possible.

It is critical that we as individuals are the ones who set the standards for what our success is going to be. You will find that your standards are always going to be higher than other people's standards for you. If you can hit your standards, then you're going to satisfy not only yourself, but everybody else concerned.

We all know a salesperson that has made more money than she or he can ever spend, yet they keep working harder than ever. What's their secret?

Successful salespeople just love what they do. Successful anybody loves what they do, because in order to be successful you have to love what you do. The most successful people in any walk of life in any occupation are usually the ones that are putting in more time, energy, effort and commitment into their jobs or their businesses than anyone else.

If you don't love it, what makes you think you're going to be willing to put in that time? You won't. So, I think the love of what they do drives them more than anything. Do what you love, because you're going to have to do it a lot in order to be successful, and in sales, I think you'd better love selling, you'd better love what you sell, because if you don't, that comes through also. And, so the love of it spurs you to want to do it because when you love it, it stops being work.

Career Happiness

Number two is what I call career happiness. What does career happiness mean? It means that you work a job that you really, truly love. If you ever worked a job you hated, you know that it's a total mental prison. To be successful, you have to love what you do. In order to be successful in a career, in order to be successful in business, you have to be willing to put in an inordinate amount of time, energy, effort and commitment towards your career or your business.

If you don't like it, you're not going to be willing to do it. I used to work in the garment center in New York City. I hated it. Not because I wasn't making money, I was making pretty good money. But because I hated it, I wasn't willing to put in the time it would take to be truly successful in this job.

I knew I had to find something I loved. I knew that if I really loved it, it would only be a matter of time before I was making more money than I ever made before in my life. Because when you love it, you're going to be good at it; you're going to do it all the time.

A successful woman I know was asked, "What is the key to starting your own business?" And she said, "Very simple. Just find something you love to do, and do it all the time. And just keep doing it. Even if you've got to give it away for nothing. And, you'd better love it because you're going to be doing it a lot." That's career happiness.

I have to emphasize how important it is to look long-range. If you are going to love what you do, don't you think that you're going to be good at it? Because you're just going to outwork everybody else. Most people don't look long-term because they have no goals. When you have no goals, when you have no plans, you're always looking at the short term. But we never look long term and say, if I work hard at it because I love it for the next three years I'll be making this much more. The willingness to take the step back to go three steps forward is scary.

A few years ago I was reading the Sunday *New York Times,* an article in the Real Estate section about real estate in the New York City area. It described how housing was so expensive in New York City that the suburbs were moving further and further away from New York. There were locations 70, 80 miles outside of New York City that were now considered suburbs that people were moving to just to get affordable housing in the New York City area.

They interviewed one young couple living in a town called Great Neck, only about twenty miles from midtown Manhattan. A young couple in their mid-20s, who was living in this town, renting an apartment, really loving this town but deciding that even though we really love this town and would love to buy a house here, we can't afford it so we're going to leave.

I read that, and thought why do you have to leave? Just because you can't afford something today, does that mean you can't afford it tomorrow? You're young. Does that mean your income is going to go down or up? Up; that's right. But they never took that one step back. It was almost like saying we'll never be able to afford it because we can't do it right this second.

That is called instant gratification. So they left, and they moved to one of those affordable suburbs in Pennsylvania. And the interview continued, "Well, what do you think?" And the young man says, "Well, it's great. We've escaped the rat race. It's quiet. I see the trees, I hear the birds."

Let me tell you how far away from the rat race he got. He now commutes 3.5 hours each way. He leaves his house at 5:00 in the morning to get to work by 8:30. He's got to drive 45 minutes just to get to the railroad station. He's got to leave work at 4:30 just to be home by 8 at night. I read this and I said, "When does he see the birds? When does he see the trees? It's always dark. How does he know they're there?"

He didn't escape the rat race. He just made it worse. When you have an attitude that you want to be a 40 hour a week worker, get in at 9 and get the heck out of there at 5, and I don't care about anything else, 40 hour a week worker equals one thing; survival. That's the best you can hope to do. The best you can ever hope to do by putting in 40 hours a week is getting by, is surviving. It is those people that put in those extra 5, 10, 15, 20 hour weeks that become successful because every time you do that, every time you put in that extra time; that 5, that 10, that 15, that 20 hours; that's an investment. That's an investment in your future.

When I read this and I said this guy has boxed himself in a corner. Here's someone willing to put in a 15-hour day. The problem is, seven hours of his day is spent commuting. Why didn't he take a step back and think this way? I'm willing to put in a long day. If I commute one hour each way for a total two hours, and work 11 hours a day, that would be a 13-hour day and I get an extra 2 hours of sleep. If he was willing to work 11 hours a day for a few years, maybe he could have afforded the house he wanted in the place he wanted to be in.

But now he's locked in to a 40-hour week because he can't work anymore than that because he's got to be commuting for seven hours. So, here's a guy who at a young age locked himself into survival because he wasn't willing to take that step back to look long range, to set a long range goal. You always have to look long term. You can't make your decisions based on short-term implications.

One of the best things you can do when it's time to make a decision is ask, if this was the perfect world and money were no object, what would I do? And that will help you to decide what to do with your life. That's career happiness; finding something you really, truly love. Finding something that makes you want to go to work every day. The money is not the motivator. When you're really, truly doing something you love, you just don't ever want to stop doing it. That's career happiness. Career happiness is critical to our well-being. We have to love what we do in order to be a success.

What if I'm really not that unhappy with my job, but I know things could be better and that I could be happier? Is there anything that I can do to put some spark back into my job? This brings us back to the question of communication. Many times people get unhappy with their jobs because they're not getting the tools that they need to do the job properly. Or they're not getting enough variety on their jobs. Maybe because they're not getting a chance to do other things on the job to add a little diversity and just do something different.

If this is the case you have to go to your boss. You have to be honest. You have to talk to people. Many times our managers, our bosses, don't know what's going on with us unless we open our mouths. In other words, if you don't ask you don't get. And, if you're not getting the tools you need to do your job better, or to do your job in order to make you happier about it, then you've got to open your mouth.

Tell people, this is what I need to do the job more effectively. Or, what can I do to put some spark back into this job? Or are there any other things I can do in conjunction to my job that would just give me something new and something fresh to do? I think you've got to do that, because your manager or your boss is not necessarily looking at that, and it's not their place to volunteer it. It's your place to make it happen.

Let's talk about putting in long hours in order to be successful. Is this really critical to success?

Putting in long hours is critical to success, but I don't think that stands alone as being critical to success. You do have to work hard, but it's just as important to work smart. I'm sure you know as well as I do that there is a difference between working hard and working smart.

A lot of people work hard, but they never seem to get anything done because they have no focus, they have no direction, they have no goals, they have no set plans. So, the only reason they're working hard is because they're so busy spinning their wheels and going off in a million different directions. So, while working hard is critical to success, you really have to work hard *and* work smart.

Working smart is first taking that step back and fig-uring out where you want to go and how you're going to do it and then go out and work hard to get it.

To be successful, you must do what you love. This is the motivating factor that will enable you to work the extra hours and take on the additional tasks that will make you stand out in your career, yet loving what you do, working hard and working smart, is not enough. You can't do everything yourself. You need help. You need support from your family, friends, managers and asso-ciates.

Family Happiness

The third area of concentration for creating a happy life is what I call family happiness. What is family happiness? Does that mean you're married and you have children? Not necessarily. But what is does mean is that you have a sense of the fact that you cannot do it alone. You cannot be successful all on your own. That pull yourself up by your own bootstraps theory is really good, but it doesn't go far enough, because you need help.

Everybody needs the support and help of other peo-ple to make it. No one makes it on their own. Whether it be your spouse, or close friends, or other people at work, it's the sense that you have that crew of people that you can always count on when you need them, and in turn they know they can always count on you when they need you. That is true family happiness, because nobody does it on their own.

One of the things I always tell people who are about to make a career change, starting a new job or are about to go into their own business, and, especially if they're married is, "Your first and most important sale is at home." If you can't close the sale at home, don't bother, because you're going to need that support. If you're going to start a new job, if you're going to start a new career, if you're going to start a new business, you'd better get 2000% backing at home, because the world is going to be rough to you when you first start out.

When you come home, you don't need it being rougher. So, you need that support at home. I was very lucky. When I made the decision to start my own business, I went home, and talked to my wife about it. I walked in the door with the decision that I was going to start my own business; this was about six years ago. I'll never forget what happened. I said to her, "I've decided I'm going into business for myself." It would have not have been unusual to hear things like, "Are you sure this is the right time?" Or, "Can we afford this now?" Or, "Did you think this thing through?" Or, "Well, it sounds like a good idea. Tell me more about it." My wife looked me right in the eye and all she said was, "It's about time."

What could stop me when you've got that kind of support? How can you be stopped? Yes, the change is scary, but you're always going to need that support. You can't do it alone. You'd better have that support at home.

I've met a lot of salespeople and small business own-ers who are facing this, saying: My husband doesn't understand or my wife doesn't understand. Yes, I just started this job, I'm a salesperson, and I've got to be out late every night going to see people. I'm on late appointments, I work late hours and my husband doesn't understand, my wife doesn't understand, they want to know why I have to be out late every night. That's a real drag on someone who's starting out in a career.

One piece of advice I always give to people, is to bring that person into the process. One of the first things I did when I started my own business was to take my wife with me on a road trip, on a particularly rough one. We drove about 120 miles, we stayed overnight in a crappy motel and I mean crappy.

The next morning I did a full day seminar, finished speaking for a full day, hopped in the car, drove another 50 miles and did a dinner talk. Finished that dinner talk about 10:30 at night, got back in the car, drove all the way home about another 100 miles. The next morning my wife woke up and she said, "You know, all I did was sit in the audience and I'm exhausted. I can't imagine how you feel."

But that gave her a real good understanding of what it is that I do, and what it is that's going on when I'm out there late and when I'm working every single day. Bring your spouse into the process, if you need that support. Take them out on some appointments with you. Let them see what it is that you do. Let them see that you're out there working; you're not sitting in some coffee shop somewhere. You need that support, because when you come home after a rough day, you're going to need somebody in your corner 2000%.

That's true family happiness. The other part of family happiness is at work. You're in sales, you think you do it alone? No, you don't do it alone. Sales people don't do it without marketing, marketing doesn't do it without product development, you don't do it without the sales support staff, without the secretaries. Everybody in your office needs everybody else.

I don't care how big or how small the link in that chain is, if you break it; it's not a chain.

I want you to think about this. In most big companies, who is the only person who speaks to every single customer? That's right; the receptionist. Think about that. The only person who speaks to every single customer is the receptionist. And how do most companies treat the receptionist? And that receptionist is speaking to every one of your customers.

What if your biggest customer calls and no one answers the phone? Good-bye. That customer leaves. The beauty about being a customer is that the customer votes with their feet. They can leave you. You need other people.

To strike a balance between our personal lives and careers, we need other people. We need a family that understands what we do and supports us. And we need that support and understanding at work. We need to be able to count on our sales manager and co-workers to help us make that all important sale, or to help us keep our customers happy.

Key Roles in Sales Support

There are a number of support areas that are very important in selling and it's hard to say that one area is more important than the others. However, it's always been my opinion that one of the key links in the chain is the sales manager. That is such a key position, illustrated by that old expression, the fish stinks from the head. If you give me a bad sales force, and a top-notch sales manager, I guarantee you within six months to a year, you're going to have a top-notch sales force. On the other hand, you give me the best sales force in the company with a lousy sales manager, and soon you will have one bad sales force.

I think that the key and critical support base for the salesperson is his or her sales manager. The sales manager is there to support the salesperson, to give direction and to reinforce training.

Training

Training is one of the most critical things for sales performance and I believe it is incumbent upon the sales manager to find ways to deliver training to the salesforce, not necessarily personally, but most likely through professional development. And equally important is the follow up, reinforcing the training, to ensure that the salesforce is able to put into practice the valuable tools they've learned. When I do sales training seminars, I always ask the manager, even demand of the manager that they sit in on the session. Nothing I do is going to work unless that sales manager is also there, hearing what I'm teaching their salesforce. They now have the opportunity to reinforce the training, which is the key.

If I do a great sales training session, and the manager does not reinforce what I taught the sales force, then it just all crumbles. They don't act on it. So, the key is, after I leave, that manager has to be able to take what I've given the sales force and reinforce it on a daily, weekly, monthly, and yearly basis.

Much of what I cover is how to consistently give direction and support to the salespeople. For a sales manager, his or her sales force, is that sales manager's customers.

The sales manager's most important job is to support the sales force. This not only includes reinforcing training, group direction, and establishing goals for the department. It also includes taking care of problems, especially problems that pertain to getting the products off the shelf and to the customer.

Here's an example from my days in the garment store. We had a head bookkeeper who tough, critical and always expecting the worst. We had a shipping room, where we shipped the dresses from. The people that worked in the shipping room were minimum wage employees and likely illegal immigrants.

There was also an invoice clerk, or charge clerk. All he did all day was hand-write invoices. We probably shipped out fifteen thousand dresses a month. He'd stand there in this dusty, dirty, airless shipping room, writing out invoices all day. The most boring job you can think of. He was in one spot the whole day.

This charge clerk rarely made a mistake, but whenever he did, that head bookkeeper would just jump on it. She'd run into my office with that invoice and she'd throw it on my desk and say, "Here, look at this, what I'd tell you about those people." Finally one day I'd had it. And she came in with one of those invoices and said her bit. I said, "Sylvia, you're right. You're absolutely right. They're no good. So I'll tell you what we're going to do. Right now, I'm going to walk downstairs to that shipping room, and I'm going to fire everybody."

She's looking at me like I'm crazy. I said, "No, no, don't worry Sylvia. Don't worry. It's okay, because even after I fire them, understand something, you and I, we're geniuses, right?" "We're high-paid geniuses. We never make a mistake. I know you never do. So, what we're going to do is, at 5:30, when the day's done, you and I, we're going to go down to the shipping room, and we'll do all of the shipping and invoicing ourselves. What do you say? Sylvia? Oh, Sylvia?"

That was the last I ever heard of her. Let's understand this, we need other people. I don't care who you are, I don't care what you do, I don't care how successful you are, have ever been, or will ever be. You need help. And, once you start to understand that, once you start to understand that you can't do it alone, once you start to understand that you need that core around you that you can always count on them and they can always count on you, then you've achieved family happiness.

Mental and Physical Happiness

The fourth area that I want to talk about is what I call mental, emotional, and physical happiness. Mental and physical happiness. This is pretty self-explanatory. It means you're healthy. It means you have your peace of mind. I think that's very important and it has become a big thing. There was a big birth of entrepreneurship in the 80s. People were starting up businesses left and right. And even more so, women were starting up businesses left and right, three to four times faster than men.

When they did surveys of female entrepreneurs, to find out why they were starting these businesses, they discovered that money had nothing to do with it. Maybe one or two percent said money was the motivator. What did they want? They wanted control. They wanted that peace of mind. They wanted the ability to achieve and to be as successful as they could possibly be.

In corporate America, many women can't rise above a certain level. So these women were saying, "Well, hold it. I want to rise as far as my talent and my ability will take me, so I'll start my own business." or, "I want to be able to live the lifestyle I want to live. I have children, I want to be able to have a career and see my kids at the same time, so I'll start my own business and let my kids sit in the office." "I want to be able to have control over my life. I want to be able to have control over my creativity. I want to be able to have control over my ability."

That's why they started businesses. That's why most entrepreneurs start businesses. Money is not the motivator. A lot of them start their businesses because they have a great idea, and they want to fill a need that they perceive society has. And because of all of those other attitudes they have, they make the money. The money is just a by-product of your attitude, of your commitment and of your action. That's what true mental and physical happiness is. That's where it comes from. That's why people do the things they do. For that peace of mind.

That's what's happening now in the 90s. How many business magazines have you read where people are not going on the fast track anymore; because they realize that there was not that much to it? *Fortune* magazine and *Business Week* have done a number of articles about this. How people are literally taking lateral moves within their companies, because they want to be able to spend more time with their families. They want to be able to change their lifestyle. They are more interested in lifestyle now than they are in the fast track. That they've found that they worked hard towards the fast track in the 80s and now they find that there was something missing. They didn't have that sense of balance. They didn't have that sense of control, and they want that now. That's mental and physical happiness.

The fast track of the past has given way to the concern for more control over our life. We're no longer interested in just forging ahead without enjoying some of the benefits of our hard work. The way to achieve some balance in our life is to take control of it. And don't we in sales have more freedom than in other professions to be in control of determining what our lifestyles are going to be? Isn't it up to us to determine what our goals are and then to go out and get them?

If you really think that you're a good salesperson, and you really enjoy selling, why wouldn't you want to be on commission where you never have to ask a boss for a raise? You never have to worry about how much money you're going to make. And, you can set your own rules. You can make as much money as you're capable of making. You can reach your own level of achievement without any kind of barriers, and I think that you do have more control over your life. You almost set your own hours.

Being an outside salesperson you never have to go to the bank at noon. You never have to eat lunch when everybody eats it. You never have to be on the highway when everybody else is on the highway. There's just so much freedom in what you do, that yes, I think it's just so much better than most other professions as far as the freedom aspect is concerned. Salespeople really have the best of both worlds, working for a company and essentially working for themselves.

It does take that entrepreneurial mentality to succeed in sales. I think it takes that kind of mentality to succeed in almost any job. We have conducted surveys of top producers or top earners, and when I say top producers or top earners, I mean people who are employees of a company. In these surveys, the top people felt that they were working for themselves. And I think that is a very important attitude, because when you're working for yourself, and you have that attitude that I'm working for myself, and the person I have to please more than any-one is myself, then I think you'll be a lot more productive and a lot more successful because when you can please yourself, you'll end up pleasing everybody else because you are, without a doubt, your own harshest critic. And, if you're your harshest critic, and you can please yourself, then you'll please everybody else.

In sales, you essentially are working for yourself. You're out there every single day, and no one can tell you you're doing a bad job if you're doing a good job, because your score is up on the board every single day. On the other hand, if you're not doing a good job, you can't convince anybody that you are, because again, the beauty of sales is that you score is up there on the board every single day. So, you always know how you're doing.

The true definition of success says that you must be able to reach a high level of happiness in all areas of your life. This includes having control over you mental and physical happiness, gaining support for family happiness, committing the time and energy for your career happi-ness, and establishing your level of financial happiness. But, there's also the area of spiritual happiness. That is, understanding the positive impact you make on other people's lives.

Spiritual Happiness

Let's go to the fifth area of concern, which says, you have to achieve a high level of happiness in a spiritual area. Now, what does that mean? Does that mean you're a religious person? It could, but it doesn't necessarily mean that. Let me tell you what spiritual happiness means.

Spiritual happiness means that you have a true sense of who you are. You have a true sense of your own self-worth. You have a true sense of your own identity. You have a true sense of the fact that you make a difference. That you make a positive impact on people's lives. That if you were not around, it would have left a void.

That's very important to feel. That's very important to understand. There are a lot of people that have real problems in their lives because they never understand that, because they never feel that way. They never feel that they're making a difference. You really have to understand that you do make a difference.

In Rabbi Kushner's book *When Everything You Ever Wanted Isn't Enough,* he found that the single biggest reason middle-aged men ended up in therapy was they didn't feel they were making a difference. That they didn't make an impact.

He looked at men from all walks of life. They just didn't feel they were making a difference. They just didn't feel that they were making a positive impact on people's lives, and that's why they ended up in therapy.

Here is a terrific example of that, the movie, *It's a Wonderful Life.* You must have seen it. It's on TV every year, all the time between November 1st and the day after Christmas. This is a movie about spiritual happiness. Think about it.

Jimmy Stewart played a fellow named George Bailey, who Bailey lived in this little town, called Bedford

Falls, and he wanted to do great things. He wanted to travel the world, build things, do great things for people, but because of family circumstances, he got stuck in that crummy little town running the family business.

Remember the family business? The crummy little Bailey Building and Loan. Think about it. What was the Bailey and Loan? They were building middle-class, single family housing. That's what they were doing. And, he was stuck in Bedford Falls running that crummy little building and loan, and because of certain financial setbacks he was having a real hard time, and then he got into some serious financial trouble, because of his drunken uncle, Billy, and because of this serious financial trouble, he decided everybody would be better off if he would just kill himself.

He decides to commit suicide, but since it's the movies, he has a guardian angel, and the guardian angel said it's really stupid to kill yourself, and George Bailey insisted everybody would have just been better off if he had never been born.

And, of course, since it's a Frank Capra movie, and you've got a guardian angel, you get to see what would have happened if you'd never been born.

And, what did he find? He found that while he might not have done some of the great things he wanted to do, he found that many people who had come in contact with him, and because they had come in contact with him, had gone on to do great things. He had changed the course of people's lives, through the impact he made on them. And remember what the angel said, the angel said, "It's amazing how many men's lives touch other's lives." How many other people's lives we touch. Remember that.

Do we think about that? Do we ever take that step back and think about how many other people's lives we really touch? We do. Remember one of the last lines in the movie, his brother toasts him, "To my brother George, the richest man in town." Remember what happened? The whole town came by and all gave them money. But, you see, that's true spiritual happiness. That sense of the fact that you really do make a difference. That sense of the fact that you do touch other people's lives in a positive way and that if you weren't around, it would have left a void.

Now, what is true success? Well, true success is when we can reach a high level of happiness in all five of these areas. When we can create that balance in our lives, and it's very important, because, if we let any one of those five get out of whack, it could literally drag the other four down with it.

Think about it. Have you ever known anybody who made a lot of money, had a fantastic career, owned a big business, and all of a sudden one day went through a terrible family problem. Have you ever known anybody like that? A divorce, a really rough divorce or bad custody case, and haven't you always found that it always dragged down the other areas of their lives? That everything just kind of fell apart. Have you ever noticed that? One thing happens to someone, a terrible tragedy, and things just fall apart.

One of those things could just drag everything down. It happens to us in minor ways, every single day. For example, if you have young children and have ever gone to work on a day when one of your kids was home sick with something minor, like a 24-hour virus. Is your mind fully on your work that day? No way. Your mind is partly at home. In fact, you probably called home 12 to 14 times. Here's something minor that can affect the other areas of your life that day. So we can see how something major is really able to just drag everything down?

That's why we have to reach that high level of happiness in all five areas. That's why we need to not just set monetary goals; to not just set career goals and business goals. Rather, we have to set goals in all of those areas.

They all intertwine. They all overlap, and unless you've got everything in balance, everything at a high level of happiness, then you'll never really reach the success you want to reach.

What do we do when one of them gets out of whack?

You know if any one of those five areas does get out of whack, it is going to drag the other four down with it. That's when you have to really start working hard in your life. It's easy to get everything in balance, harder to keep it in balance; I think that's when a person really has to start working hard on their life.

You have to work on your life all of the time. I really believe that. This doesn't come easy. Success is not an easy thing, but I think when something gets out of whack, whether it be a family problem, an emotional problem, a physical problem, or even a monetary problem, I think you have to first sit down and really start to work on that problem without sacrificing every other area of your life.

I think, too many times, what happens to people for instance, if someone's going through a bad business problem, I think they tend to forget their families and leave them out of the loop, which is very natural; it's hard not to. Though in a situation like this, that's when you look to bring those people even more into the loop because you need their support more than ever. If I was having a bad business problem, I wouldn't separate my family from it, I'd bring them into it because maybe they can help me get through it, even just with their own emotional support.

In other words, instead of letting that one area that gets out of whack drag down the other four, we're using the other four to try to prop that one area back up again to where it should be in order to create that balance all over again.

How can salespeople can use this spiritual message from *It's a Wonderful Life* in their jobs?

I have a saying I love to use. It's called "Successful salespeople don't sell, they help." Their attitude is, I cannot help you, unless you first see me, and once you see me I cannot help you unless you buy my products and services. Because you see successful salespeople really, truly believe that what they do helps their clients. If they believe that their products and services are the best in the market, the attitude then becomes it is my obligation to make sure I get you to buy this from me. Because if I believe that what I have is the best, and I allow you to go buy from my competition, then what am I doing? I'm allowing you or helping you to buy second best.

And, if I help you to buy second best, am I not doing you a disservice? And so, if I really believe that what I have is the best, it's absolutely my obligation to walk out of there with the sale, because I really, truly believe that what I'm doing helps you as a client; makes you more successful in your own business; and maybe helps your company become more profitable.

I always take that attitude, when I sell my services as a speaker. I really believe that if people do not hire me, they lose more than I do. That I can always walk down the street and go find another client, but they can't go find another Warren Greshes, because I really, truly believe that what I do helps the people I do it for, and I really believe that I make a positive impact on my audience and help them become more successful.

So, I think salespeople have to always take the attitude that they don't sell, they help. And, if they just keep helping all the time, people are going to want to buy from them because people want to come to someone who helps them.

The True Meaning of Setting Goals

What I'm really asking you to do in these five areas is to define what you want out of life.

I don't want people to just set monetary goals. I don't want people to just set career goals. I think that in order to create that balance in your life, you have to set goals in all five of those areas. You have to set spiritual goals. You have to set emotional and physical goals, and family goals, that everything intertwines. Everything overlaps everything else.

Let's face it, when we have a bad day at work we bring it home with us. We have a bad night or a bad day at home, we bring it to work with us. The whole idea is to set goals in each one of those five areas. Only by doing that, can we finally define how we want our lives to look.

Developing a balanced life of financial, career, family, mental and physical and spiritual happiness is just a start towards a successful life and profession. You need to be willing to do whatever it takes to achieve your goals in each of these areas of happiness.

Obstacles to Success

I want to talk about now, why people don't do all the things they know they should do. I've talked about commitments. I've talked about attitude. I've talked about setting goals, the importance of having a sense of purpose in your life. The importance of having a plan and a set of goals, and I always notice that when I talk about and speak about all this stuff, people sit in the audiences and they all bob up and down. They nod their heads, oh yes, he's right; oh yes, this is nothing new; absolutely that's what you've got to do.

The question is, if you know I'm right, if you know it's got to be done, if you heard it a million times, then how come you don't do it? Any why don't people do it? I want to explore what I find to be the two biggest reasons why people don't do all the things they know they should.

Fear of Failure

The first one is fear. Fear of failure. The single biggest reason that people do not succeed is because they are afraid to fail. Fear of failure is the single biggest obstacle to success.

Let me tell you something right up front, it's okay to be afraid. It's okay. We've been taught to believe that it's not okay to be afraid. It's okay to be afraid. You know what's not okay? It's not okay to let the fear stop you, that's what's not okay. Everybody's afraid. Change is scary, I said that before. No one likes change. No one likes the unknown. Heading into the unknown is a scary thought, it's a scary task, and it's natural to be afraid. But, it's not good to let the fear stop you.

I'll never forget a couple of years ago I was doing a talk to a group of MBA candidates at New York University, and we were talking about all sorts of business topics, motivational topics. And near the end of my talk a young man raised his hand and asked me a question, when you started your business and you wrote your business plan, what was your contingency for failure? Typical MBA question, right?

And I looked him right in the eye and I said, there was none because failure never crossed my mind. Why would I do it if I even thought about failing? Why would I even attempt to start my own business and say, "Well just in case I fail," that's like a self-fulfilling prophecy? But how many people do that in their lives? How many people attempt to change their lives by holding on to something you want to let go of? How many people enter a business and say well, if I fail I can always go back to my old job?

I hate it when I hear people say, well, I'm just going to do it part time. I'll keep my regular job and I'll do this part time and if it works out I'll leave my job. You can't be successful part-time. Successful people are not successful part of the time. Successful people are successful all of the time. And just remember, you cannot cross to the other side of the river if you keep one foot on the side that you're starting out on.

Did you ever play on those hand-over-hand bars in the park as a kid? The only way to get there is to eventually let go. You can't get to the other side if you keep one hand stuck on the first bar. You eventually have to let go of that first bar. But the fear of failure, the fear that we're going to fall stops us because we've been conditioned to think that failure is a terrible thing. We have been conditioned to think that falling down is a terrible thing. Falling down is not a terrible thing, what's a terrible thing is not getting up. Doesn't matter how many times you fall, if you keep getting up.

Just remember successful people do all the things that unsuccessful people are unwilling to do. You got to be willing to break away from the pack. You got to be willing to do things that everybody else is not willing to do. You've got to be willing to be different if you want to be successful in life, if you want to be successful in your careers. You've got to be willing to separate yourself from your competition. Why should I deal with you if you're just like everybody else? People amaze me. I can set my watch by the human race.

The highways are crowded the same exact time every single day. Everybody gets on the road the same exact time every single day, and what do they do? They sit in their cars in traffic, and scream and yell to themselves how much they hate the highway. I hate this road, oh man, this road's always so crowded every single day, I can't stand it, I hate sitting in this traffic, and what to do they do the next day, same thing. Same exact road, same exact time, same exact traffic, and same exact complaints.

And you know what, folks, in most cases all you've got to do is change this much. Make one small change. You just have to make that little tiny change. Small changes implemented on a consistent basis will always yield you great results. Maybe leave 15, 20 minutes earlier in the morning. Maybe go home 15, 20 minutes later at night. But no, most people will sit in traffic and complain about it.

Another thing you can set your watch by, people's banking habits. I love watching people go to a bank on Friday afternoon so they can have the pleasure of standing on line at a bank. And they stand on line and they yell and scream and moan, "Oh, I hate this bank, the line is always so long. Look at it, there's 40 people in line, there's only two crummy tellers, I'll never get out of here, I'm never going to get to eat lunch, my boss is going to kill me, I hate this bank, the lines so long, it moves so slow."

And the next Friday at noon, what do they do? There they are, standing on line complaining about the line. By the way, think they knew on Monday that they needed the money? Oh, yes. And then Tuesday, Wednesday, and Thursday, but they waited till Friday, got on line, and complained about it. Because they just weren't willing to change that much, that little extra bit. You know most people say, "Well, people get paid on Friday." Okay you get paid on Friday, do you have to cash your check on

Friday? Well, sure they have to cash the check on Friday. If they don't they won't have any cash for the weekend.

So because you won't have any money for the weekend you keep the same routine going, week after week for the rest of your life, when all you had to do was change this much. Just take one weekend and don't leave the house. Isn't it worth to take that one step back, give up that one weekend just so you can now go to the bank every Monday? Just change the routine and not have to stand in line.

People stand on line, complain about the lines. And people are so resistant to change, so worried about what might happen. We've been conditioned to think that failure is such a terrible thing. So what? It was just another experience in your life. So what? We value our experiences. We learn from our experiences. But we're always told, don't step out of the way, don't do anything different, don't try to go beyond the crowd.

What about multiplexes, those movie theater complexes with 20 screens. The entrances all look the same. They have four or five sets of double-glass doors. Did you ever watch when the crowd files out? There are four or five sets of double-glass doors, so literally you have eight to ten doors. Now none of them are locked, but only one is swung open, the one all the way to the right, and 200 people file out of a movie theatre and they all go to this one little opening on the right and they're all trying to squeeze through. When all you'd have to do to break away from the crowd is this much. Take one little extra step to the left, and exert some effort.

It's that way in life. Just break away and exert some effort. But most people don't do it. Why? Well, what if I break away from the crowd, what if I push the door and it's locked? Because remember folks, if all you choose to do with your life is to follow the crowd, all you can ever hope to be is one of the crowd.

We've always been told that if we fall down that's the worst thing that could possibly happen to us. No, the worst thing that can possibly happen to us is that we don't get up. We've been so conditioned to believe that failure is terrible. No, it's not. And you don't fail if you keep going. You only fail when you stop.

There was an article recently in *Wall Street Journal*, it was really an incredible article. They interviewed educators, they interviewed teachers, I should say, on what their new policy is on leaving kids back in school. And they talked about the fact that they used to believe leaving them back in second or third grade, but now they don't believe in leaving them back in second or third grade because they think it's no good for their self-esteem. So if a kid fails second or third grade they just pass them onto the next grade.

Oh, that's good for their self-esteem. Kid can't do second grade work so let's make him a third grader where he can really get buried. If he can't do second grade work how you going to expect him to do third grade work? And, if you put him in the third grade where he's really going to get buried, what happens to the third graders who can do the work, but who have to sit around while all the attention is given to a kid who can't even do second grade work?

And they say, well it's a bad stigma to put on a kid to leave him back because he failed second grade and I thought about it, I said, why did he fail? He didn't fail. Did the kid fail? No he didn't, he just didn't pass second grade. You know when he failed second grade? When he drops out of school in second grade, that's when he failed.

But if you get left back in second grade and you go back that second year and you pass second grade and get promoted to third grade, did you fail? No, you just didn't pass it on the first time around. But they call it failing. Those kids didn't fail; they just didn't pass the first time around. There is such a stigma that if we try something once and it doesn't work out we failed so we're just better off giving up.

What about the driving test? Many people do not pass their driving test on the first go around. The road test, that parallel parking gets lots of us. When I ask my audience did you pass your driving test first time, I often hear, "It took me a year." Many people would say they failed their driving test. No, you just didn't pass it the first couple of times, that's all. You're driving. You've got a license. That's not failure, that's falling down.

Yet it never ceases to amaze me how we just put the tag of failure on these things. In that article about the kids getting left back in school, my favorite was the last paragraph. In that they interviewed a teacher and they talked to her about, you know, why don't you leave these kids back if they can't do the work? You know what she said? She said, "Oh yes, well how many adults get back up again and try harder after they've fallen down?"

And I read that and I said, only the successful ones. She's right. Most adults will fail, fall down, and not pick themselves up. Only the successful ones will keep going. Isn't that an incredible attitude? You don't fail if you keep getting up. Don't be afraid folks. Don't worry. It's okay to be afraid. Don't be afraid to fail. It's okay to fail, too. It's just not okay to let the fear and the failure stop you.

In sales we all have to deal with fear when we call on a new account or ask for the order.

Well the biggest fear in sales is the fear of rejection. Most salespeople are afraid someone's going to say no. And the truth is, they're right. So how do we deal with the rejection, because that's the biggest problem? Many salespeople don't sell, don't call on potential customers, out of fear of rejection.

The only way to handle it is to know just how much rejection you need. Again we come back to planning. We come back to setting goals. We come back to keeping records. We come back to writing things down.

If you keep records as a sales professional, because you are a professional, then you will know how many dials of the phone you have to make to get someone on the phone. You'll know how many people you have to speak to on the phone to get an appointment. You'll know how many appointments you have to go on to close a sale. You'll know how many sales you have to close in order to make the amount of money you want to make.

So if we know all our ratios, if we know all our numbers, we'll know how much rejection we need in order to make that sale. Once we know how much rejection we need, it becomes that much easier to swallow the rejection and a lot of the fear is then taken out of it.

Risk taking is a big problem for many sales reps because they're afraid of falling down and having others see them fail.

But isn't it true that and worry less about others seeing us falter? I don't think that it really matters whether anybody notices or not. I do think that many people are concerned about what everyone else will think, which is why they never do a lot of the things they want to do with their lives. By taking little risks we overcome our fears and the important thing is to take those little steps, so perhaps the falls aren't as big and they don't hurt as much so that we'll be more willing to get up.

The whole idea is to only do as much as you're capable of without getting sick of it, without changing the habits so drastically that you're not going to want to do it anymore. Because remember the biggest thing we worry about is giving up. It's okay to fall down, it's just not okay if you fall down and never get up.

So the whole idea yes, you take those little steps, so that you build more and more confidence. Confidence only comes from the doing. It's the commitment that gives us the courage to act, to take those little steps. And once we've taken those little steps and found out that we can actually do something, only then do we start to develop the confidence. And once the confidence builds, we start to take bigger and bigger steps, and we don't worry as much about falling. We're more concerned with succeeding than with failing. That is how we become successful.

Habits

Now let's look at the second thing that stops more people from being successful than anything else. Very simply, that's all those little things you know you should do, but you don't. That's all those little things that we just can't seem to change. The procrastination, we just can't seem to get out of bed at certain times, we just can't seem to get going every day. We just can't seem to get that paperwork done. We just can't seem to make those calls.

And what are those really? What do we call them? Habits. It's all those habits that stop us. All those conditioned habits that we've developed over the years that stop us from being successful.

You know why people don't change habits? Not because they don't want to, we all want to. We all want to change those bad habits. It's not a matter of wanting to or not wanting to. The reason we don't change the habits is simply because of the way we go about doing it.

There is a difference between a habit and an addiction. An addiction, is smoking, drinking, drugs. The only way, or the most successful way I should say, to cure an addiction is very simply, cold turkey. You just have to stop.

Those of you that have ever quit smoking know it is extremely difficult or almost impossible to quit smoking by cutting back, that the easiest and fastest way to quit smoking is to just stop doing it cold turkey. I used to smoke, I finally quit. And I used to try to quit by trying to cut back. I was one of those people that said I can quit whenever I want, I've done it a million times. Did you ever do that? You smoke a cigarette and then you sweat for 53 minutes. You sit there staring at your watch and waiting. No, you have to stop.

The difference is this. The way you change a habit is totally opposite from the way you change an addiction.

Most people try to change a habit cold turkey, by stopping. The only way to change a habit is a little bit at a time because that's the way you acquired it. That is the problem, we try to change our addictions by cutting back. We try to change our habits by going cold turkey.

People say to me, I know I procrastinate a lot, but I'm going to change. I've been procrastinating for years, but Monday morning I'm going to come into work with lists and I'm going to get all my paperwork done the second I touch it. Every piece of paper I touch for the first time I'm going to get it taken care of, and I'm going to go from being the world's number one procrastinator on Friday to being the world's most organized person on Monday.

Forget it, you can't do it. If you try to go from one end of the spectrum to the other in one shot, what's going to happen? You're going to hate the change so much because it's so drastic. You're going to hate it so much you're just going to give up.

It's like losing weight, everybody figures that they have to lose all the weight all at once because they all believe that's the way they put it on. You didn't. The only way to lose weight is a little bit at a time because that's how way you gained it. And you know 97% of everybody who loses weight gains it back and more because of the way they lose it.

You know why those crazy diets don't work? They don't work because the change is too drastic. People go on these crazy diets, I've got to lose 21 pounds in 13 days so I'm going to go on the grapefruit and dust diet. You can lose the 21 pounds, but let me ask you a question. After 13 days of eating nothing but grapefruit and dust, what are you going to do? You're going to go nuts. You're going to have a potato chip frenzy. It's the same when you go on a diet where you just eat the same thing, a delicious shake for breakfast, a delicious shake for lunch.

How you going to eat a shake for breakfast and a shake for lunch every day for the rest of your life without wanting to kill somebody? You'll walk past the pizza place and you'll eat them out of business. Because the change is so terrible, how do you feel about dieting? You hate it. You hate it so much you're not going to do it.

My favorite is those people who say to me, "You know I have so much trouble getting up in the mornings. I just can't roll out of bed. I want to get up early, I want to read the newspaper, work out, eat breakfast. I want to get my paperwork done, to get to the office; I just can't get out of bed."

"Well, what time do you get out of bed in the morning?" "Oh man, by the time I roll out of bed it's always 9:30." "What time do you set your alarm for?" "Five."

"Five?" You know those people that hit the snooze alarm every seven or eight minutes for the next four hours, do you know how tiring it is to sleep in eight minute intervals?

And I ask, "Are you nuts?" "Yes, but you don't understand, I want to read the papers every morning and I want to eat breakfast, and I want to run four miles." "Yes, but you're getting up at 9:30." "Yes, but I want to get up at five." And I say, "But you can't. You can't make that kind of drastic change."

How can you do it? Tomorrow set your alarm for 9:15. When it goes off at 9:15 get out of bed. Now that's not what you wanted, but it's 15 minutes better than you'd been doing. You do that for a month, and then you know what, next month set your alarm at nine. And when it goes off, get out of bed. Do that for another month and set your alarm at 8:45. When it goes off, get out of bed. Do that for another month, 8:30. Just keep doing that.

One of the biggest problems with salespeople is that they hate calling because it's all so much rejection, so they never call.

When you ask a salesperson, "How many calls did you make last week?" And they say, "I know, I know, I didn't make enough calls." "How many calls last week?" "I know, I know, I didn't make enough calls." Right away I know the answer, three. That's it. Three telephone calls. Three people said no and that was it.

"I know that's not enough. From now, on starting next week, I'm going to make 100 calls a week." I say, "Do me a favor, and don't bother." "Don't you want me to make more calls?" I say, "Sure I do. But I don't want you to quit after one week. If you're a salesperson making three calls a week and then all of a sudden you're going to move to 100 that's an extra 97 calls. Which means for someone used to making three calls, you're now going to be swallowing an extra 90 pieces of rejection a week. After the first week of they will be dragging you off in a straightjacket. So I say, "You're doing three a week now. Do you think you can handle five calls a week?" "Sure." And they always say sure, no problem. "Good. Next week make five calls. Make five calls and when you get to five stop. Do that for a month. At the end of the month if five is easy, go to seven. Do that for another month. At the end of that month if it's easy go to ten. Make ten calls a week for a month."

Keep increasing every month, little bits at a time. The whole idea is to build up to a hundred, but gradually. You're not going to build a person up to a hundred by forcing them to do something that's unnatural for them, by forcing them to do something they're going to hate; because basically, we don't do the things we hate.

One of the things I hate that sales manager do, and that is phone-a-thons. "Alright, everybody, Monday nights, we're all coming in and we're going to spend all Monday night making calls. But I'll give you a free piece of pizza. Oh, whoopee! Monday night phone-a-thon, I want you all on the phone making a hundred calls each."

By Sunday night how does everybody feel about the phone-a-thon? They dread it. People are dreading Monday night and here they are getting on the phone trying to do business, doing something they dread. What kind of attitude is coming out over that telephone? That can't be too good.

I would much rather see you make ten calls a day, every single day, rather than fifty calls once a week. Make the same 50 calls a week, but you'll develop the habit. If you make 50 calls a week just once a week, you will never develop the habit. You will just start to dread that one day you have to make the calls. If you do ten a day every single day, it will just start to flow. It will become part of your normal routine. Remember, the key to changing habits is always, a little bit a lot; rather than, a lot a little bit.

Identifying Bad Habits

Before we can change our bad sales habits, we need to be able to identify them. Sometimes that's not so easy. How do we go about pinpointing those activities that are making us nonproductive?

How do most professionals identify their bad habits? For example, let's take a professional athlete, a baseball player, a top hitter. You know what they do? They watch videotapes of themselves constantly. They keep a videotape of themselves of almost every single at bat, and when they're in a slump they go back to the videotapes that show what they were doing when they were hitting well, and they go back to the tapes that show what they were doing when they were hitting poorly.

How many salespeople have any kind of records, or any kind of catalog of what they were doing when they were going well and what they are doing when they're going badly? Once they get into a slump they have no idea how to get out of it.

I recommend salespeople keep records, call counting sheets, ratio sheets, showing what your normal ratio of dials to contacts is, what your normal ratio of contacts to appointments is, what your normal ratio of appointments to held interviews is, and what your interviews to sales is, or your closing ratio is. Then if you find, through your records that you're in a slump all of a sudden, you know exactly the area that you're slumping in and you can start to ask yourself, why would this happen?

For instance, if I noticed that it was taking me a lot more dials to get to the decision maker, I can ask why is this happening. I can look back in my records and find that I started to call at a different time of day; that I was calling people when they were out to lunch, or I was calling people when they were already gone for the day, or when they weren't even in yet; rather than the optimum time of day to call. Record keeping for the salesperson, much like videotapes for the baseball player, is not only what's going to help us get out of slumps, it's going to help us to avoid slumps altogether.

Not asking for referrals

In order to get referral business you always have to be aware of three key points. There are three things you have to do to get referrals.

Number one, you have to ask. No one is going to just volunteer a referral, so you have to ask for a referral.

Number two, you have to ask for a specific number of referrals. In order words, I just cannot say, "Could you just give me the names of everyone you know?"

But if I said to you, "Could you give me the names of your three best friends?" You could certainly do that. But many salespeople don't do this. They say things like, "Well could you give me the names of anybody who might need this product or service?" This doesn't frame the question. A better way to frame the question is "Could you give me the names of three other people you know who might be able to use my product or service?"

The third thing you need to do is not only ask for a specific number, but you need to ask the kind of questions that can be answered. For example, if I am working with a business owner who is my client, I know one thing. I know that most people know and hang around with people much like themselves. So if I'm with a business person who owns his/her own business I would ask, "I know you've gotten a lot of value out of my products and service, would you be able to give me the names of three other business owners that you are friendly with who might also be able to use my products or service?

Do you see the difference? I framed the question, I asked for a specific number and I gave that person a question that they could answer. If I was with the vice president, I would say, "Do you know three other vice presidents who might be able to use my services?" So, always ask for specific number and ask the kind of questions that clients can answer.

If we fear failure, we're never going to have the opportunity to experience the thrill of success. The successful salespeople are the ones able to get up after they fall down. They are able to take fear for what it is, a challenge. And they know how to make the changes necessary for getting out of their bad sales habits by doing a little bit at a time. Now that we understand what gets in the ways of our achieving success, we need to know the most important tool of all; learning to set goal for success.

We've talked about commitment. We've talked about attitude. We've talked about the importance of a high level of commitment, and the importance of having a fantastically great attitude, beyond a positive attitude, but just a great attitude. And, we've talked about the importance of goals, and having a sense of purpose in your life and in your career.

The Five Step Process

I want to take you through a five step process that I developed that will help you to focus in more clearly on what it is you want to achieve in your life, and in your careers, and in your business that will get you to the point where you will walk out of here with the beginnings of your own written five year plan. And, the five step process will help you to focus in on what your goals are, and what you want to achieve in your life and career, when you want to achieve it by, and how you're going to get to that point.

See It

The first step in the goal setting and planning process is that you have to be able to see it. You have to be able to see yourself successful, because if you can see yourself successful, you can *be* successful. If you can see yourself doing something in your mind then you can do it, but if you can't even see yourself doing something in your mind, then how can you possibly expect to be able to do it in reality?

Have you ever heard anyone say, "I can't imagine doing that in my wildest dreams?" If you can't do it in your wildest dreams, what makes you think you can do it in real life? You know as well as I do it's a lot easier to do stuff in our dreams.

See it. See yourself successful. Visualize it. What you're trying to do is to create a picture in your mind of what you want your success to be. We think in terms of pictures. We don't think in terms of words. We don't see numbers or words in our minds, we see pictures of what we want and what you're trying to do is to create that picture of what you want your life to look like, of what you want your success to be. See it, visualize it, and create that picture in your mind.

Actually visualizing our dreams in detail and seeing them come true is the first step of the goal setting and planning process. Everyone who's ever been successful has been a dreamer. If we look throughout history, throughout any industry, throughout any profession, it's always been those people who had the ability to dream the big dreams, and to act on the big dreams. It's not just a matter of dreaming the big dreams, but to take those dreams, and put deadlines on them, and to formalize them as goals, and to breakdown a plan to get them—who have been successful.

But it always starts with the dream. Everything has to start with that dream, like a Steve Jobs, putting together a whole new concept for computers out of his garage. Don't think that Steve Jobs didn't start with a dream that became Apple computer. I mean, here was some guy in his garage tinkering around with computers. Probably in high school, you would have called this guy a nerd, but he had a dream of a whole new technology and that new technology started out as a dream.

Martin Luther King has a speech called, "I Have a Dream" and his success was based on his dream that he had. Anybody who's really been truly successful, who has gone on to make incredible achievements in life, in business, in any walk of life, has started out with that dream, and has gone and followed that dream.

Watch out for Excuses

Dreaming by itself is not enough to achieve our goals. We also need to follow through with action. Too many times we let excuses for not taking action get in the way of accomplishing what we want out of life.

I want you to all think about this person that you know because you all know someone like this. You know an excuse maker? Those people that always tell us how successful they could have been, but they never have any luck. They don't get any breaks. Nobody likes them. They're always telling you that everybody's always plotting against them. They don't have any connections.

We all know people like this. In New York City, we have a saying. "Everyone in New York knows somebody else who could have bought a building 30 years ago for

$9." You're walking down the street with this guy, he says "See that building over there?" "Yes." "Thirty years ago I could have bought that building—$9." "Well, why didn't you?" "Ah, those lousy jerks, they talked me out of it." "Why don't you buy it now?" "Nah, it's too late now."

You know what? They're right. It is too late. For them, it's too late because they believe it's too late. But, now just for the moment, let's say the excuse makers are right. Let's say they're right even though we know they're wrong. Let's say they have no luck, never catch a break. Nobody likes them. Everybody's always just plotting against them. Let's say they're right. I still have one question for all the excuse makers. How come you still could not even see yourself successful?

Think about this. Nobody stops you from dreaming, and if you don't have good dreams, the only thing that's left is nightmares. So, see it. See yourself successful. Visualize it. Create a picture of what you want your success to be in your mind.

As I travel around the world, one of the most distressing things that I find is how few people I actually come in contact with who seem to be able to see themselves successful. Most of the people I run into seem only have a capability; to see themselves failing. That is why I am tired of people saying to me how bad business is, of hearing about the recession. I am tired of salespeople saying things like, nobody's buying. Nobody's buying.

Are we to believe that nobody, anywhere, at any time is buying a single thing, at all, ever? I know you're thinking, "That's not what they mean when they say it." Perhaps, but remember if you say something long enough, loud enough, and hard enough, you start to believe it.

Let's think about it. Nobody's buying. I first started hearing when the recession was kicking in. At the end of the year I said, "Nobody was buying this year. Gross National Product was $5.3 trillion." Someone had to buy something that year. Then next year it got worse. The economy took a turn for the worse, and they really weren't buying. It was so bad that the Gross National Product went down 1%.

Yet in that year when absolutely, positively, no one was buying, somehow $5.2 trillion worth of business magically appeared. I think every one of you would settle for the 0.2. I know I would. That's even more than a lot. You see, I am convinced that the single biggest reason that people do not do business during recessions, and the single biggest reason people do not do business during tough times is that they simply give up.

The recession becomes a convenient excuse to not have to do business. The average person walks into the office that day, they pick up the phone, the first three people they call say, "Nobody's buying." They hang up the phone and go, "I'm covered. I'm covered." Now, if my boss wants to know why I'm sitting around doing nothing all day, I can say, "Well, you know it's tough out there, nobody's buying."

It's because they're listening to all those other people telling them how bad it is. Don't let those other people stop you. Folks. Because they want you to stop. They need company. They want you down there with them.

I'm not going to sugar coat it for you. I'm not going to tell you things are great out there, you'll know I'm lying. They're not. Yes, it's tough out there. It's harder to do business now than it's been for a long, long time.

I don't care how tough it is. I don't care how tough it's ever been, and I don't care how tough it's ever going to be. Somebody out there is always doing business. Why shouldn't that somebody be you? But, how many people are so busy listening to all those other people telling them how bad it is that they just give up.

Don't let those other people stop you. They're ready, they're willing, they're able, and they will. I know what I'm talking about. Because at one time in my life, I let them stop me.

My first sales job, ever, started off in July of 1973. I got a job selling dresses for a dress manufacturer in New York City's Garment Center. I spent ten years selling dresses in New York City's Garment Center. In the dress manufacturing business they had a saying, "You can't do business in December." Every industry has one of those sayings. Every company has one of those sayings. I call them the, you can't do business in, sayings.

Some people say, "Oh, you can't do business in December because everybody's getting ready for the holidays, and they don't want to talk to you." Or, "You can't do business in January. No one's going to talk to you in January because they've got no money left over from the holidays." And, certainly, "You can't do business in the summer. Come on, nobody does business in the summer. Everybody's getting ready to go away on vacation."

"You certainly can't do business on a Friday. Come on, no one does business on a Friday. Who's going to talk to you on a Friday? They're all getting ready to go away for the weekend. And, you certainly can't do business on a Monday. No one wants to talk to you on a Monday because they just got back from the weekend." In fact, I'm convinced there's this one Wednesday in May that's the only good time of the whole year to do business.

Well, in the Garment Center, they got this whole group that's convinced you can't do business, and we all have those people. Years later, I came up with a name for those people. I call them the coffee cup brigade.

Do you know why? Do you ever notice these people? You work with them. They don't do anything all day but pontificate. They know everything, but they never do anything because all they're really busy doing all day is walking around pontificating with a coffee cup in their hands telling you how bad it is.

In the Garment Center, the coffee cup brigade is not only convinced that you can't do business in December, but they're afraid to even try.

"No one's going to buy anything in December to bring in in January because January's clearance month.

All they want to do is get rid of stuff. Nobody buys a dress as a Christmas present. Dresses are not a Christmas item. If they have any dresses in stock, all they're going to want to do is return them." They say, "Don't even pick up the phone because if you pick up the phone it's only going to be a complaint." In fact, the saying goes, "It's so bad in December even the hangers don't fit."

And, here I was. December, '73, just turned 22. It was my first December ever in the dress business. I didn't know you couldn't do business in December. Nobody ever bothered to tell me. So, me like a dope, every morning I'd come in early, I'd pack up a bag with samples, and I'd run out into the market. I'd spend all morning visiting buying offices in Manhattan, and I'd stop for a quick lunch, come back to my office, open my bag, hang up my samples, sit down at my desk, and all afternoon I'd spend calling department stores out of town.

I was so young, so dumb, so naïve, I kept doing business, but don't worry, because you know what happened next. It's happened to all of us. I heard the voices. You know the voices?

We've all heard the voices. Those ones that are always so ready, willing, and able to tell you it can't be done. I heard them going, "Hey, kid, come here." That's how they sound. Really. They all think they're racketeers in the Garment Center. There they were, under their desks with the coffee cups.

"So, what are you guys doing under there?" They said, "Are you crazy? You can't do business in December." I said, "You can't?" They said, "No. Nobody does business in December." I said, "They don't?" They said, "Don't you understand, no one's going to do any business in December; nobody's going to buy anything in December, bring it in December because the store's already stocked for Christmas. Kid, are you a dope?"

"No buyer's going to buy anything in December, to bring in January because January is clearance month. All they're going to do is get rid of stuff. Kid, nobody buys dresses as a Christmas present. A dress is not a Christmas item. If they have any dresses in stock, all they're going to do is return them." They said, "Kid, don't even pick up the phone." I said, "Why not?" They said, "Because it's only going to be a complaint." In fact, they said, "Kid, it's so bad in December even the hangers don't fit." I said, "Oh, man."

Don't worry, folks, because by the next December, I knew. I was now one of those veterans. You know who I was? I was now one of those guys who knew what he was not supposed to know. I had officially enlisted in the coffee cup brigade. You see, I now knew that you couldn't do business in December. And you know what? I didn't because I listened to all those other people.

Don't let those other people stop you. They want to because if they stop you they have company. And, it's always a lot easier for them to bring you down to their level than to get off their rear ends and move forward with you because in the long run nothing is always the hardest thing to do.

Watch out for negative influences

One of the things I've found you have to be able to do is to just stay away from all those negative people, as much as possible. Sometimes, it's just not possible. Sometimes they exist in our own homes and in the workplace, but wherever you can, I think you've just got to cut those people out of your life because I don't think they're doing you any favors. They're stopping you from being successful.

When I first left the Garment Center and would run into somebody who was still there, there'd always say the same thing. "Boy, you're so lucky you got out. I wish I could, but you know I can't." And, I would actually stand there with them and argue that they could; that I didn't do anything anyone else couldn't do, I just did it, and that they could do it too.

I'd get so frustrated standing there trying to convince them they could do it, and it would just bring me down. I finally decided that what to do when someone says, "I wish I could do it, but you know I can't." Or, "Hey, that's a good idea, but it can't be done." I just look at them right in the eye and I say, "Yes, you're right. You can't do it." And I walk away.

I found it better to avoid listening to the losers and to stick with the winners. The only thing you're going to learn from losers is what not to do. Of course, you want to stick with the winners. That just makes sense, and in fact, it's not only a matter of sticking with the winners, but of watching what the winners do, and how they got to where they are, and doing that.

I think every person who wants to be successful needs to find a role model. Again, that's one of the good reasons for setting goals. If we can decide how we want our life to look, if we can decide how we want our success to look, then we can go out and find somebody who's done exactly what we want to do. When we find that person, we should make them our hero, or our role model, and find out, not only where they are now, but where they were when they were at the same level we are at, and how they got from there to where they are now.

When I speak to top producers, one of the questions I always ask them, "Has any young salesperson come up to you recently and said "Listen, I'd like to learn more about how you became successful. Could I get a few minutes of your time? Maybe have some coffee, have some lunch, and ask a few questions and pick your brain." And, most of the time I find out that those top people are never being approached. What a waste of an opportunity, that is, for someone starting out as a salesperson.

We can all learn from the successful sales pros, and one of the most valuable lessons is that they keep plugging away. They're out there doing business, no matter what the excuse makers are saying. I know it's tough out there. I know it. I know it's tougher out there than it's been in a long, long time, but like I said before, I don't care how tough it is. I don't care how tough it's ever been, and I don't care how tough it's ever going to be. Someone out there is always doing business simply because they believe that they can.

They see themselves successful. So, see it. See yourself successful. Visualize it. Create that picture of your own success in your mind, and once you've seen it, once you've visualized it, once you've created that picture in your mind, focus in on that picture. Focus in clearly until you can see every single detail of that picture, until you can take every single detail in that picture and describe it.

Write It Down

Now that you have done that, created that picture of your own success in your mind, once you have seen it, once you've visualized it, once you've focused and described it down to its most minute detail, we are now ready for step two of the goal setting and planning process which is "Now that you can focus and describe exactly what it is that you see in your mind, you've got to write it down."

Why? Well, very simply, let me ask you a question. Did you ever wake up in the middle of the night with a good idea? And said I'll remember it in the morning. We get an idea, we go back to sleep, we wake up in the morning, we forget it. And maybe next time, you wrote it down. What happens? You look at the paper and it reminds you, and maybe you come up with some other ideas, and now write them down as well.

It works. When we write it down, we get up in the morning we see it, we get excited about it. This is reason number one to write down your goals. Very simply, if you don't write them down, you're going to forget about them. It is that simple.

Why else should you write down your goals? The very simple second reason to write it down is that the writing down of a goal is your first commitment to doing it. You all have goals. You all have dreams. I'm talking about the big stuff, those big goals, those big dreams.

You know, as well as I do that those big ones, they could take you as much as two, three, five, ten years of time, energy, and effort to achieve. If you're not willing to take ten minutes to write it down, what makes you think you're willing to take ten minutes to go out and get it. That's the second reason to write down your goals.

And, the third reason to write them down is because the writing down of the goal makes you accountable to the one and only person that you can never fool—you. Let's be honest. You can fool anyone you want: you can fool your husband; you can fool your wife; you can fool your boss; you can fool your parents; you can fool your children; you can fool your teachers; you can fool your coworkers; you can fool anyone except you can't fool yourself.

You are the only one that knows the absolute positive truth. And once that goal is written, it's going to be real hard to look at yourself and admit you did nothing about going after it. If it's not written, it's out of sight, out of mind. If it's not written, you don't have to admit you did nothing to go out and get it. That's why a lot of people don't write down their goals. They let themselves off the hook, so to speak.

If they don't write it down, they never have to admit they didn't do everything possible in their lives to get what they really truly wanted out of their lives, and now they have that ability to complain about it. So, the first reason is, if you don't write it down you forget it. Second reason, it's your first commitment to doing it. The third reason to write down your goals is it makes you accountable to the one and only person you cannot fool.

Let me take it a step further because I know lots of people in your life have told you to write down your goals.

Write down what you want, focus and describe. I'm sure you hear that all the time. People hear the same stuff all the time from the same people or from different people, and it like goes in one ear and out the other.

I have this very strong belief, that comes from working in the Garment Center. I have found that no matter what you're selling in this world, whether it's tangible or intangible, the best way to sell an intangible is to always make it as tangible as possible. One thing that I have learned is it's a lot easier to let people buy into what you're selling if you can let them touch and feel the merchandise. If you can, make that sale as tangible as possible, no matter how intangible it is. That's why I take those dollar bills. I could stand up here until I'm blue in the face and tell you, you got to ask. I'm sure other people have done that to you.

But, you're never going to forget the fact that I took money right out of your hand, and the next time you're sitting in on that sales call, and it's just about to come to the close, all of sudden in your mind, you're going to see that guy taking that dollar bill out of your hand and you're going to say, "If you don't ask, you don't get." Because I made it tangible, I made it visual.

So, let me show you in a tangible, visual way that you can relate to why you should be writing down your goals. Let's talk about going food shopping, real food shopping on a semi-regular or regular basis, and have you ever gone food shopping with a list? Now think about going without a list. We've all gone shopping with a list, and without a list. What's the difference?

You don't buy what you need, when you're shopping without the list. Without the list, you also forget stuff and you buy more things you don't really need or want, and you waste time and you waste money.

When you go out there without a focus, without a direction, and without something written down, without some sense of purpose, goal and plan written down, you end up wasting money, wasting time, getting a lot of things you don't need, and still not coming back with what you really wanted and needed. By the way, did I mention anything about food shopping there?

When you go out there without a list, you always end up wasting time, you always end up wasting money, you go off in a million different directions, you take on a lot of things you don't need, and you don't seem to get what you want. Isn't that incredible?

So many people don't write down their goals; you ever notice that? They don't write down their goals. I don't have time to sit down and start writing this stuff down; I've got to go, I've got to do, I'm just so busy. You know, I'm busy, I don't have time for this. I've got to go, do, I've got a million things to do, and they're always off in 14 different directions. And when you go off in 14 different directions at the same time, you never end up anywhere.

Do you know any of those people that are just so busy, but never get anything done? You know what I call them? Human gerbils. Think about that. Have you ever watched a gerbil? A gerbil is, without a doubt, the busiest little sucker in the entire world. He gets on that wheel and he just goes while you're sleeping. And when he's done, he lies down on his side, panting, because he's just so busy. He never gets anywhere, never leaves the wheel, never leaves the cage. So many people are like that; they're unwilling to take that one step back, invest that little bit of time upfront to get that huge return in the backend.

Did you ever notice that when you go shopping with a shopping list how focused you are? Your shopping just flows and you go from one aisle to the next, boom, boom, boom, and you move through that store like that.

And when you go without a list how, how you always seem to be running from one end of the store to the next? You start out over here, you grab something, and oh, geez, I forgot something, and you've got to run all the way to the other side of the store. Oh, where'd I put my wagon?

Did you ever notice something else about shopping lists—can you make up a shopping list by aisle? My wife can do that. You make up your list and you know where everything is. Have you noticed that you're visualizing where everything is? You're visualizing where everything is in every aisle. What are you doing? You're seeing yourself successful. And did you ever notice how when you go shopping after making up that list by aisle how the shopping just really breezes right through?

And that is because you've already done it in your mind. It's not the first time you've gone that day; it's the second. The first time you did it, you did it in your mind. That's why it went so fast the second time. You already knew where everything was because you'd already been there.

But did you ever notice that when you go without the list you always seem to buy the same things that you didn't need the last time you went without the list? Things like peanut butter, eggs, and milk? You stand in front of the peanut butter shelf saying I know I've got that at home. I know I have a jar. I'm sure we have some at home. No, I think we just ran out last week. No, I know we have it. And you stand there for 15 minutes debating whether you have peanut butter or not and finally you go oh, what the heck, I'll just buy another jar. And you get home and what happens? There are three jars in the cabinet from the other three conversations you had with the peanut butter jars.

Now, let's take it a step further. We'll admit that in the larger scheme of things and how it relates to your life and to the priorities in your life that grocery shopping is relatively irrelevant.

I want to show you how, when we really focus and put together a sense of purpose and direction in our lives, how it really comes back to us. How, when we take that step back, to take that little extra time to plan it out, how we end up taking three steps forward or ten steps forward in something as irrelevant as food shopping. Let's look at this.

Let's analyze shopping with a list versus without a list. First, how long does it take you to write out your shopping list? Let's say ten minutes.

Now, how long does it take to do the shopping? I'm talking from the time you walk out the door of your house, get in your car, go to the super market, do the shopping, put the bags in the trunk of the car, get back in your car, drive home, unload the bags—how long does that whole process take? Let's say an hour and a half.

Now, when you go without a list, how much time would you estimate you waste? How much longer does it take you, let's say, without the list? That's likely to mean an extra half an hour. That's conservative; I want to be low.

Next, how much extra money do you blow when you go without the list? That could be an extra $30, which sounds pretty conservative. Okay, $30.

Now let's look at this. When you're willing to take 10 minutes up front to write it down and plan it out in something as irrelevant as food shopping, within only an hour and a half, you are saving yourself 30 minutes. That willingness to take that ten minutes up front is within an hour and a half getting you a 300% return on your investment in time and putting $30 in your pocket that you didn't have. This is for something as irrelevant as grocery shopping. Could you imagine what kind of return you might get if you did that with your life?

That's why you write down your goals. That's why you take that step back to write it down, plan it out, which allows you to take those ten steps forward. If you want to be successful in life, you've got to be a long range thinker. You can't make your decisions on short term decisions. You can't think short term.

Knowing this, here is an exercise for you to do. Take a clean sheet of paper and draw a straight line across the top of the page. And on the right side of the line, write down today's date. And on the left side, write today's date minus five years. Now, along this line, plug in the most significant things that have happened to you in the past five years. It doesn't matter what it is; you can put down anything you want, whatever you consider significant. Just think of the most significant things that have happened to you in the past five years and write them along that line according to the year that it happened.

Now, go back over those things that you've written down, and draw a circle around any item that you had either direct or indirect control over.

All of them? Bingo. It's likely you circled all of them or all except maybe one or two. Guess what folks? You're in control. You control your life. You control your destiny.

There are a lot of people that don't know that or don't believe that. There are a lot of people that know it and refuse to believe it. Why might they know it but refuse to believe it? We come back to accountability because if they believe it and they admit they believe it, they have to also admit that they're accountable. They have to also admit that maybe they didn't do all the things they should have done to get what they wanted out of their lives and their careers.

But whether you believe it or not, now you know it. Because you have that piece of paper in front you, because I have made it tangible. Because you can now touch and feel the fact that you control your life and you control your destiny. And if you're not going to believe it somewhere down the line, carry that piece of paper with you, and if you're ever in a situation where you stop believing that you're in control, pull that piece of paper out of your pocket, open it up, look at it, and realize, I really am in control. Because you control your life and you control your destiny. Whether you believe it or not, it's happening. Whether you believed it or not in the last five years, it was happening.

So now, knowing this, knowing that you control your life and you control your destiny, here's what you're going to do next. Take another sheet of paper and draw another straight line across the top of this page. On the left side of the line write today's date, and on the right side write today's date plus five years.

Now that you know that you're in control, that you control your life and you control your destiny, I want you to plug in the most significant things you would like to see happen to you in the next five years.

Hold it. The last one was easy because that's already happened. That's gone. There's not a lot we can do to change that. There's a little criteria now because this is the one we really have control over. Because now we know we have control, so now that we know we have control, we have even more control to make it happen.

Three criteria before you start writing it down. The first thing is this: when you write down what you want to see happen to you in the next five years, please be specific. Don't write down next year I want to make a lot of money.

Number two is timeframes. When you put down what it is you want to see happen to you, plug in the year you want to see it happen, because a goal is nothing more than a dream with a deadline. There are so many people out there that tell us all the great things they're going to do in their lives and when we ask them when, they always say sometime.

And you know as well as I do that sometime doesn't exist. If you wanted to make an appointment to see me to sell me something and you called and said, "Warren, can I come over and see you sometime?" And I said, "Yes" and hung up, when would you come? Better do it right now.

Think about it; let's examine that phrase sometime. When do we use the word sometime? We use the word sometime when we don't want to do something, right? Your wife tells you to take out the garbage, what do you say? I'll get around to it sometime. When are you going to paint that ceiling? Oh, someday. Someday I'll get around to painting that ceiling. Someday we're going to clean out this garage. Someday I'm going to do this, and you know you have no intention of doing it, that's why you say someday. Because someday never comes, right?

Did you ever run into someone on the street who you didn't really dislike, but weren't that crazy about, and if you never ran into them again, it wouldn't have really mattered that much. But you run into that person and there's no way of getting around it and you never were really friends and all of a sudden you say, how are you? It's so good to see you. You look great; you lost weight.

You know, they always lose weight; everybody's always losing weight. You look great, you lost—you know we never—we should get together sometime. Right?

Give me a call sometime. How long you in town for? Oh, you're only in town through tomorrow. Oh, too bad, I'm leaving tomorrow. Well, the next time you're in town, give me a call, you'll come to visit us someday. In fact, don't even call, give me your number, I'll call you sometime.

We use the word sometime when we don't want these things to happen. What are we saying when we talk about our goals and say we're going to reach them sometime? We're saying we have no intention of making them happen. Let's underline timeframes. When you plug in what you want to see happen to you, plug in the year you want to see it happen.

Number three is very important: please, don't place any limits on your ability to achieve. If it's what you really want, put it down. Don't place any limits. Don't rationalize your life away. Don't say this is what I really want but I don't believe I can really get it and since I don't really believe I can get it I will settle for this.

The second you say to yourself I will settle, that's as far as you're ever going to get, because you have just placed a glass ceiling over your head. And you'll get as far as that glass ceiling and you'll spend the rest of your life looking through that glass ceiling on what you really wanted and you'll spend the rest of your life saying, I know I never could have gotten that, so I'm really kind of happy where I am now, and that's okay.

I don't believe in realistic goals. I don't believe there's such a thing as realistic goals. People say set realistic goals. To me, realistic is a code word for low.

In other words, they're telling you don't set a goal unless you're absolutely, positively sure you can achieve it. Don't even set a goal if you're not 100% sure you're going to make it. Set your sights low. Don't set your sights too high. Don't ever try to stretch yourself. Be realistic.

What's realistic? Was it realistic when Madonna decided she wanted to be Madonna? Was that realistic? People must have thought she was out of her mind. Oh good, yes, you're going to be a star, sure. Oh, great idea, walk around in your underwear. Good, lots of people will go for that. They did. Was that realistic?

People are always trying to prove me wrong. They say, okay, sure, you say I can have anything I want? I'll tell you what, next year I want to make $10 million. Fine. Is that realistic? Isn't it? Haven't a lot of people in this world made $10 million in a year? Someone's doing it. In fact, more than someone's doing it. You know when the reality sets in? When I then tell you what you're going to have to do to get it. Then, all of a sudden, you'll say oh, that's not realistic. Oh, no, I don't really think I need the $10 million. You don't want to do what it's going to take, it's not that it's unrealistic.

It's like someone who could say well, I want to be a major league ball player; I can't do that, I'm 35 years old. Why not? Sure you can. That's realistic. But you know what's not realistic? When I tell you what you're going to have to do to get it. You want to be a major league ball player at 35 years old? Tell you what: you married? You got kids? Forget them, because for the next ten years, you're going to play baseball every single day. That's going to be your job.

You're going to give up your job. You're going to play baseball and practice baseball every single day for the next ten years and you know what? You're not going to get paid to do it. Because those kids, when they're nine years old that decide they're going to be professional baseball players, they play and practice every single day. They give up their social lives, they give up everything for the next ten years, and they don't get paid to do it.

And after those ten years, you know what you're going to get? You're going to get to sign a great minor league contract. And when you're 45 years old, you're going to have the advantage of making $500 a month, riding rickety buses and eating crappy, greasy hamburgers for the next 5 years. And then, maybe, you'll get to be a major league baseball player. So, you ready, pal? Well, you know, I don't think that's too realistic.

It's not the goal or the dream that's realistic; it's what you're going to have to do to get it. Be specific, set timeframes, and place no limits on your ability to achieve.

Now, back to your timeline, I want you to plug in the most significant things you would like to see happen to you in the next five years.

Remember what I talked about before? See yourself successful. As you're writing these things down, try to visualize it. Try to create a picture in your mind. It becomes a lot easier to be specific if you can think of it first in a picture, and then translate it to the paper.

Do you have any idea what you have just done? You made a commitment, you focused, you started the process, and you set some goals. And do you know how long it took you to do this? Seven minutes. That's less time than it takes you to make your shopping list. But everybody's so busy. And what you've just done is more than 99% of the people out there will ever do in their entire lives. You've just put yourself ahead of 99% of your competition. All you've done is started the process, and I believe in starting slow. I believe in making small changes.

I'm not telling you that everything I'm saying is absolutely, positively right and that you must do it. What I'm saying is that over the course reading this book, I'm going to give you a lot of good ideas. If what you're doing is not working 100% to your satisfaction, here are some ideas.

Give it a shot. What have you got to lose? If what you're doing is working 100% to your satisfaction, keep doing it. But, if what you're doing is not working 100% to your satisfaction, and you're not willing to try some new ideas, then you do lose.

I'm hoping you gain just a little different perspective. Maybe it's just that willingness to try something a little bit different. I don't want you to change overnight. I don't want you to change everything; you don't have to. I just want you to change that little, tiny bit. Because I know that small changes, implemented on a regular basis, will always yield great results.

So start off slowly. Those of you that aren't used to goal setting, that have never really done this before, don't think you must become goal setting experts. I don't need you to do that; you don't need to do that. Just be being willing to try it. If you're willing to try it, and you like it, you'll keep doing it. Just don't give up, because if that happens, it's really over.

So start off slowly. Go back over those goals you've written down and pick out three that you want to work on, more than any others, and put a number one, a number two, and a number three next to those three goals.

By placing no limits on our ability to achieve, we keep our horizons open. Here's an example I'd like to share with you, one I love to talk about because I happen to know this person.

I was speaking at a convention in London, and met a young man who is a life insurance agent in London; his name is Peter Rosengard. I'm sure nobody knows who Peter Rosengard is, but Peter Rosengard is in the Guinness World Book of Records for selling the largest life insurance policy ever. He sold a life insurance policy with a death benefit of $100 million on the life of David Geffen to MCA Records.

Why is this significant? Let me tell you the story, because it has a lot to do with someone who did not limit their expectations and their ability to achieve and went far beyond what people would think were their own limits.

It seems that one day, Peter Rosengard was reading the newspaper, and he saw that MCA had just acquired Geffen Records for something like $600 million. MCA is one of the largest entertainment companies in the world, now owned by the Matsushita Corporation out of Japan.

Peter knew something about the music business, and the first thing that occurred to him was that Geffen Records, while it was a good company, was really just David Geffen; that he was the whole driving force behind the entire company, and that if you take David Geffen out of Geffen Records, there really wasn't anything left.

So he thought what if something happens to David Geffen? MCA's entire investment is right down the tubes. He said somebody ought to sell MCA a life insurance policy on the life of David Geffen. The average salesperson probably says something like, I couldn't think of doing that. It's MCA; they probably have 50 guys on the payroll that have already taken care of that for them.

Peter Rosengard never once thought of that. He just thought I have a good idea, I have a dream, somebody should sell them a life insurance policy on David Geffen's life. It would be something that they need, that the customer needs, so you know what? I'm the one that should do it. So he decides to call up MCA.

Who does the average salesperson call at this point? Probably the average salesperson calls personnel or something like that, which is the same thing as talking to the wall. Personnel normally say something like we can't give out that kind of information and they give up.

Not Peter Rosengard; he figures I'm going to the top. I'm calling Sid Sheinberg, the president of MCA. So he calls Sid Sheinberg, and what do you think happens? He doesn't get through. At this point, what does the average person do? Probably gives up, even if they've gotten that far.

He keeps calling; never gets through. But you know what happened? He got to speak to the president's secretary, and you know what I've always found? When you go to the top, and you deal with the secretary to the president of a large corporation, that person is usually the nicest person you could ever come in contact with. That's usually how he or she got to that level.

He found out from the secretary that Sid Sheinberg had left for Italy, what city he was in and she didn't know when he would be back. The average salesperson might wait or simply give up. But Peter Rosengard never assumed, never prejudged, never set any limits on his ability.

Let me back up and give you some background. Every day, Peter Rosengard has breakfast at the exclusive Carlyle Hotel in London. He meets a prospective client every morning there for breakfast. His father works at the Carlyle Hotel, so he's gotten to understand the workings of the place and he's made friends with the concierge of the Carlyle Hotel. Understand that the concierges at the finest hotels in the world are all connected and eventually retire as millionaires because, in those prestigious hotels, you're dealing with prestigious people.

He found out that all the concierges at the finest hotels in the world belong to the same Golden Key Club. Peter Rosengard had an idea. He asked the concierge at the Carlyle, "If I was a top executive, president of one of the largest entertainment companies in the world, and travelling to this particular city in Italy, what hotel would I stay at?"

And the concierge told him, "There's only one hotel to stay at." "Do you know the concierge at that hotel?" He said, "Of course I do." "Could you call him for me?" So he called the concierge at the hotel in Italy, found out Sid Sheinberg was staying there; found out the room number.

What's the next thing he's got to do? He's got to call him. What does the average salesperson do? They're going to call. At any time; they're not going to pick the right time, they're going to call anytime, probably leave a message, which, of course, will never be returned.

Not Peter Rosengard. He sat down, he thought about it. He did some preplanning. He said I know one thing about all these big shots: they all dress for dinner. Now, if I was going to be dressing for dinner, when would I be in my room to dress? Well, figuring cocktails are at 6:00, dinner is at 7:00, if I call at 5:30, I'll probably even catch him in his underwear.

He calls the room, 5:30, and what happens? Bingo. Hello? It's Sid Sheinberg on the other end of the phone. The window of opportunity has just opened one crack. Now, what does the average salesperson say when he hears Sid Sheinberg's voice? They usually say *humanahumanahumanahumana* because they never know what to say because they never planned it ahead of time.

Let me tell you what Peter Rosengard said. He said, "Mr. Sheinberg, Peter Rosengard from Abbey Life in London. Mr. Sheinberg, congratulations on that shrewd deal of acquiring Geffen records." Isn't that a great thing to say? First of all, didn't that man want to know he made a shrewd deal? Doesn't he like to hear it? Don't you all like to hear that you made a good deal?

Second of all, it was a good thing to say because what do you think the trade publications were saying at the time that the deal was made? Paid too much, made a bad deal, paid way too much money. Of course, five years later they'll be saying what a shrewd deal he made, how smart he was to get in early. It's amazing how so many people don't recognize opportunities when they fall in front of their faces.

He made his great opening, but Sid Sheinberg didn't become president of MCA because he's dumb. "Okay, what's this all about?"

And Peter Rosengard said, "Mr. Sheinberg, while the acquisition of Geffen Records was a shrewd deal, you know as well as I do that Geffen Records is really David Geffen. Now let me ask you something: what would happen to your investment should something happen to the life of David Geffen?"

And you know what the president of one of the biggest companies in the world said? "Wow. We never thought of that. What did you have in mind?" Oh, the window of opportunity just flew wide open.

Now, what does the average salesperson say at this point? What do you think they say? They probably say something like $1 million, $2 million. You know why? Because the average salesperson has no conception of big numbers. They can't think in big numbers. You know why? Because big numbers will never be a part of that person's life because that person believes that big numbers will never be a part of their life. But remember, you are talking to a man who has just written a check for $600 million. You know what $1 million is to him? It's tip money.

Peter Rosengard, is a man who places no limitations on himself. So quickly and casually, he said, "I figured $100 million would be a good start." Why not? $100 million to a man that just wrote a check for $600 million doesn't seem like a lot.

And sure enough, Sid Sheinberg said to him, "That sounds pretty good. Here's a phone number. Call this number, get in touch with this man, tell him I told you to call, set up an appointment, and let's get it rolling." And that's what they did. And a few months later, the deal was closed.

This was a man who never assumed, never prejudged the situation, had a dream, had a goal, was looking to help the customer, and never once did he consider failure an alternative. Never once did he place any limits on his ability to achieve. And that is probably why, more than any other reason, he succeeded.

Plan It Out

We've just completed the second step of the five step process. You've seen yourself successful, which was step one. You've visualized and created a picture, you focused, you described, you went to step two and you wrote it down. Hopefully you were specific, you put timeframes on it, and you didn't place any limits on your ability to achieve.

But now what you've done is you set a destination for yourself. You've written down on a piece of paper something that says, "This is where I want to end up, and this is the timeframe when I want to get there by." Now we come to step three of the process which asks, "What are you going to have to do to get from where you are now to where you want to be in the next one to five years?" Step three very simply says, "You have to plan it out."

You see, everybody that has ever been successful has had a written plan. Whether it is a general sending troops into battle, they always devise a written battle plan. A football coach sending a team out of the locker room, they spend an entire week putting together a written game plan for a game that last three hours, of which two of those hours are commercial breaks.

Business owners, if you're in business for yourself you have to have a written plan. If fact, the Small Business Administration of the United States will tell you that surveys show that the single biggest reason small businesses fail is because they did not have a written business plan.

Understand what the plan is. The plan is the piece of the puzzle that stops us from getting frustrated. The plan is the piece of the puzzle that helps us maintain the motivation every single day.

People always ask me, "I set a goal for myself, it's five years down the road, how do I stay excited about it every single day?" Well there's only one way to stay excited about it every single day and that's to plan it out so that you can have something to look at every single day before you get to that goal. So you can understand "Where are you now?" You're right here. "Where do you want to be?" You want to be right there.

There's your destination. There's your end result. Unless you put something in the middle here between where you are and where you want to be, all you're ever going to focus on is this end result.

Every morning you're going to wake up and the only thing you've given yourself to focus on is this end result. And every morning that you wake up and you focus on this end result and you're not there yet, what's going to happen? Frustrated. And every day that you get frustrated you get more frustrated. And the more frustrated you get, what's going to happen? You give up.

So what is the plan? The plan is the roadmap with all the stopping-off points in-between. The plan is nothing more than taking the big goal and breaking it down into little goals. Breaking it down into something a lot more realistic and a lot closer to us, gives us something that we can focus on every single day.

Once we develop the plan with the stopping-off points, every morning we wake up, we're not focused on the end result, we're only focused on the next step. The key is not to focus on the end result; the key is to focus on the process. Because it's the process, it's each one of those steps that we achieve. If we're focused on something that's real close, that's real achievable, we're going to get it. And when we get it how are we going to feel? Good.

Every day that we wake up and we feel good, what's going to happen? You're going to keep going. Let's face it; the fun is not in the being there. The fun is always in the getting there. The fun is in the process, folks. The fun is in the fight.

The Successful Plan

I want to give you the three components that go into making up a successful plan. Number one, a successful plan is expressed in continuous action. Number two, a successful plan is broken down into accomplishable steps. And number three, a successful plan always gives us the ability to measure our progress every step of the way.

Isn't it good to know what we have to do every single day? Isn't it great to know that before you come into work you know exactly what you have to do that day to get you that much closer to what you want? Isn't it always so much easier to accomplish what you have to do that day when you know what it is, rather than leave it so open-ended? It's always easier to do that.

Let's take the example of the salesperson. Because the problem with salespeople is they always look at everything from the wrong end of the equation. The average salesperson puts together a sales plan from the wrong side of the plan.

The average salesperson sits down at the beginning of the year or the end of the previous year and says, okay, next year if I make a lot of calls, I'll make a lot of money. If I make a lot of calls that will get me a lot sales and I'll make a lot of money, mmmm, great. Rather than looking at it from the other end of the equation.

What you should be doing is sitting down and saying at the beginning of the year, how do I want my life to look this year? What's it going to cost me to live this year if I factor in everything I want to do this year? How much are my bills costing me every month? What's my overhead? What is my family going to need to get by?

Now let's look at the extras. We want to go on vacation this year, where do we want to go, how much is it going to cost? We want to start saving for retirement, how much am I going to have to put away? My kids have to go to college, how much should I start putting away every single year now so that when they're old enough to go to college they won't have to worry about that?

And then when I've added that all up I have my number. I have my "a lots." And now as a professional salesperson I can now say, "This is what I need. Now let's go out and figure how many sales because now I can come up with the number of sales." It's a lot easier to make those sales if we know how many we need. Let me show you what I'm talking about.

Let's say as a salesperson you decide that your goal, if you have figured it out carefully, is that you need to make $100,000. There's your end result. By the end of the year I want to make $100,000 in commissions. That will give me the lifestyle I need for this year. That's my goal.

The average person looking at that is going to wake up every day and be focused on that. And every day that they're focused on it and having to achieve it they get more and more frustrated. So the professional salesperson, and hopefully you are all professionals, professionals keep records. Professionals plan.

The professional salesperson sits down and says, I don't need to make $100,000. You know why? Because I know from my records of last year my average sale put $1,000 commission in my pocket. By the way you all have an average, and your average is like your "a lot." It doesn't matter what it is, it only matters that you know what it is.

I know if make $1,000 on average, I don't have to make $100,000 anymore. I just have to close 100 sales. That's a lot of sales. That's a pretty lofty goal. How am I going to do that? Hold it a second, I don't have to close 100 sales. All I really have to do is close two sales a week.

Did you ever notice it's a lot easier to make 2 sales a week than 100 sales in a year? But then a professional says, you know it's not always 100% within my control to get a sale. So do I really need to make two sales a week? Not really.

I know that my closing ratio is one out of three. So you know what, I don't ever have to close a sale. I just need to make sure I see six people every week. Six presentations every week, oh, that's a lot easier to make than two sales, I just have to be in front of six people every week.

But you know, not everybody wants to see me. Some people actually cancel. Some people don't show up when I get there. But I also know something else; that that only happens about 25% of the time, because I've kept records. And so you know what, now I don't even have to worry about making presentations. I only have to worry about setting up eight appointments a week. That's my new goal, eight appointments, that's pretty easy.

But not everybody gives me an appointment. Some people just put me off. They won't talk to me, or even if I talk to them they come up with every reason why they don't want to see me. But I know from my records of last year, that every time I manage to speak to five people on the telephone, one of them would give me an appointment on the average.

I never have to get any appointments anymore. This is getting so easy. All I have to do is to speak to 40 people on the phone every week. Forty conversations a week.

But I just can't get some of these people on the phone, the secretary screens me out, and they don't answer their phone, or they're always in a meeting. Not everybody talks to me, but some people do.

I know most of you think that no one wants to talk to you, but some people do. And from my records I've noticed that on every three dials of the phone I get through to one person. One out of every three people gets on the phone. So really, I don't have to make $100,000, I don't have to close 100 sales, I don't have to see anybody, I don't have to get an appointment, I don't even have to talk to any of these people, all I got to do is dial the phone 120 times a week, or 24 times a day.

And that is the one thing that is always 100% within your control. You might say that sounds too simple. The biggest problem with salespeople is not the asking for the sale. The biggest problem with salespeople is they never talk to anybody. They never pick up the phone. They never have any appointments because they're all afraid and convinced that everyone is going to say no.

But you see this guy doesn't care. He doesn't care. Let them all say no. I have one goal and one goal only. I know that every day that I come to work, I know every day I walk in the door and I do this, I know every day I make those 24 calls I'm getting that much closer to my $100,000.

Now how motivated do you think that salesperson is to make the calls? Very, yes, you know why? Because it has no bearing on anything. It doesn't matter what the people say, it just matters that he does it. And he's taken a lot of the fear out of the calling because he's taken that goal and broken it down into continuous action. He's given himself accomplishable steps and he's also given himself or herself the ability to measure that progress, every step of the way.

Now let's talk about those accomplishable steps because that's one of the big keys to being successful and implementing your plan. When you break it down into accomplishable steps what you're trying to do is, you're trying to something that most people don't do. What you want to do is, you want to set yourself up to succeed every day. You want to set yourself up to succeed every day.

Most people set themselves up to fail every day. We always make it so hard on ourselves. What's that old expression? The toughest step of any journey is the first step. Well, let me ask you, if the toughest one to take is the first one, why do so many people insist on making it the hardest one to accomplish?

Why not just make it the easiest one to accomplish? If you make the first step of your plan the easiest one to accomplish, won't that give you the incentive to take the step? Won't that make it easier to take the step? Won't it take the fear out of that and change that first step?

And if we take that first step and we accomplish it, how would we then feel? We feel good, and if we feel good what are we going to do next? We're going to take another step. And if we keep taking those little small steps, we start to build up that feeling of accomplishment.

We're setting ourselves up to succeed. We're doing something every day that we know we can absolutely positively do. So by setting ourselves up to succeed every single day we're making ourselves feel better and better. We're starting to build confidence.

Everybody is so worried about confidence. Confidence is a byproduct of action and doesn't come unless you do something. The commitment to the fact that we have to do something and wanting to do something gives us the courage to act. After we do it we are now confident in our ability to do it.

It's exciting when we've accumulated all those small wins that keep us moving towards our goals, but how do we keep our momentum going and our motivation up when we run into those particularly rough spots in selling?

That is the whole point of having the plan. The plan keeps us focused. When we develop a plan broken down into those small steps that we know we have to take every single day, and we develop it into accomplishable steps, our focus then becomes not that we have to make a sale every day.

Most salespeople are so short term. They put themselves under pressure that says, "I got to sell today, I got to sell today, I got to sell today." Even though if you look at how many sales they needed to make, most of them don't have to make a sale every single day. And even though they don't, on the days that they don't they feel terrible about what they've done.

So if we develop the kind of plan that just says we have to do this amount every day, we have to talk to this many people every single day, then we only have to do what we have control over. For instance, I have a very good friend who is one of the top producing life insurance agents in all of Canada.

When I ask him what is the secret to his success, he says, "All I have to do is touch 20 people's lives every single day. Whether it be in telephone conversations, in actual sales appointments, or in just delivering the policies. As long as any combination of that adds up to 20 every single day, I know I'll be successful."

So in other words, he doesn't put pressure on himself to sell every day. He knows that all he has to do is touch 20 lives, so he never has any rough spots because he's got a long term goal broken up into small, accomplishable steps.

The small accomplishable steps generate the commitment that keeps us going even when we know we're trying something new. One of the better examples of this is learning to ski.

Do you remember the first time? You're standing at the top of that hill, likely a little scared. Why did you go down? For me and many others I know, it was peer pressure. Your friends are standing at the bottom of the hill. The other reason is that the T-bar only goes up and you get off. It doesn't go down.

So you're standing at the top of the hill, you're scared. Do you have a lot of confidence in your ability at that point? Absolutely not. But you go down. When you got to the bottom of the hill what did you say? That wasn't so bad. And what did you do at that point? Went right back up again. And you weren't quite as scared the next time, because finally you had some confidence, because you had done it. The commitment to the fact that we have to do it and we want to do it gives us the courage to go down the hill, gives us the courage to act. And once we act we start to feel confident in our ability to do it again.

That is why the first thing you want to do is make the first steps easy so that you build the confidence. You start to feel that you can accomplish anything. And because you start to feel you can accomplish anything, you're going to keep going. And once you start to feel so great about it, then you start to increase the difficulty of the steps.

The best example I have comes out of World War II. In North Africa in 1943, Field Marshal Rommel had just proceeded to obliterate an entire group of British and American forces in North Africa.

He left in his wake, two totally beaten and demoralized armies; the American Army and British Army. So totally beaten and demoralized were these two armies that these men, these soldiers, had no sense of self-worth.

They had no sense of self-esteem. They had no sense of the fact that they could do anything well.

They not only felt lousy about themselves, they looked lousy. Their uniforms were dirty. The camp they were living in was filthy, they were a mess.

Into this situation came two men. At that point in North Africa, General Patton took over the American troops and Field Marshal Montgomery took over the British troops. These two men who were so very different personality-wise, immediately instituted the same policy.

To understand this, let's think about the long term goal, which was to win the war. If they had let that stand as the only goal, could they do it? No. Because what was the short term goal? Get them to believe they could win.

If they had just stood in front of those defeated men and said "Men, from now on the only goal we are going to think about is winning. We've got to go out there and beat those guys." Forget it. They weren't going to do it. They didn't believe they could do anything.

The first thing they had to do was get these soldiers to believe that they could do something. So they set forth three criteria to meet every single day. They told these soldiers they had to do three things every day and three things only.

"When you get up in the morning you must wear a clean uniform. You have to do 20 pushups every day. And you have to run one mile. That's it. That's all you have to do." It sounds so simple. It sounds so easy.

What did they know? They knew that if they gave these soldiers tasks to do that they could absolutely, positively accomplish, how would these people start to feel after a while? They would feel good. They would feel like they could conquer the world. And that is what happened. They started to feel better about themselves.

Once you start to feel better about yourself, you start to look better. Did you ever notice that about yourself, when you wear a clean, nice, fresh shirt how everything else around you starts to look better? Because they didn't want to wear a clean uniform in a filthy camp, the camp got clean. They started to believe that they could actually accomplish something.

So now those two generals started to increase the tasks. And those men started to feel better and better and better and finally they built themselves a lean mean fighting machine. And for those of you who don't know how it ended, we won.

But you see what they did? They did not ask people to do any more than they were capable of doing. They broke it down into accomplishable steps, with continuous action. It gave them the ability to measure their progress. And when you give yourself the ability to see, touch and feel, and absolutely know that you're making progress, that's when you start to feel good.

How many times do we set out on a goal that's a five year goal? Give ourselves no ability to see, touch, or feel any progress? Three months into that goal, even though we've made 5% progress which we should have made we just don't know it.

And what do we say to ourselves? We always say the same thing, something like, "You know I have been working toward this goal three months, and I still feel like I'm on square one." Already you're getting frustrated.

Let me show you what happens with salespeople. Let me show you with my two favorite salespeople, salesperson A and salesperson B. Both A and B start off the year with the same exact goal. They both decide that they are going to close 144 sales each by the end of the year.

Each one starts the year with the same goal, same destination. Difference is B; B is one of those salespeople who says "Blah, what do I need a plan for, I don't a plan, I'm gonna go, I'm gonna do, I'm gonna wing it." He's going to wing it. He's another one of those guys who wants to wing it.

You know those people that wing it. I can't understand. Those are the same people that spend six months planning a two week vacation. They'd spend a year planning their weddings, but they want to wing their life.

Now I'm not saying there's anything wrong with spending months planning your vacation or spending a year planning your wedding, but it's wrong if you don't plan your life. I mean more people spend time planning their weddings than planning their marriages. The wedding lasts for five hours including the cocktail hour.

But you see B, he said, "I don't need to plan, no, you know me, I'll always clock in at the end of the year with the numbers, I always come in. I'm clutch."

Now A, she said something different. A sits there and she says to herself, 144 sales, I don't know. I know that s my goal, but how am I going to do this. I've got to figure out some kind if plan to do this because that's a pretty lofty goal. Well as I sit here and I look at it, all of a sudden it hits me. She decides, you know, I don't have to make 144 sales this year. All I have to do is make 12 sales a month. Same thing. But you ever notice it's a lot easier to make those 12 sales a month than 144 in a year?

Well she decides that's her plan and the year starts off. January comes, January goes, and January ends. Salesperson A, she's got those 12 sales. What does she say to herself? What does she say? "Yes, I feel good. I'm right on target. I'm exactly where I'm supposed to be." What's my new goal? Twelve. That's it. My only goal is twelve. Focus on the process, not the end result. Okay.

January comes and January goes. B also clocks in at the end of January with 12 sales. What do you think salesperson B is saying to himself? "132 to go; 132, you know I broke my butt in January and I still have 132 to go." You know why he's saying that, because what is he focused on? He's only focused on the end result; 132 to go, man.

B's glass is half empty. A's glass is half full. B is one of those people that somewhere around June is going to be saying "You know, this was very unrealistic. This was much too unrealistic, come on let's get with reality, I'll be happy with 120."

But what else is B? B is one of those salespeople who loses control; who doesn't realize that they control their lives and destiny. B is one of those salespeople that tells you all the time what a great finisher they are. You know those salespeople. "Don't worry about me, I'm a great November salesperson, I'm a great December salesperson, I'm a great fourth quarter salesperson."

You know why they are a great fourth quarter salesperson? Because they don't wake up until Columbus Day to realize they're 75% behind on quota. And they have to be a great fourth quarter salesperson or otherwise they're fired.

I have managers that say to me, "Don't worry about us, we're a great December office." And I always say the same thing, "I know you are." And they always ask, "How do you know that?" and I say "Because everybody tells me that. Because none of you turkeys wake up until Thanksgiving."

But what happens when you think like that? You create a situation where if you have one bad day in December, it equals one bad year. You see if B has one bad day in December, it ruins the whole year. If A has one bad day in December, that one bad day equals one bad day.

And what happens to B in December if all of a sudden he encounters a freak snowstorm that closes down the city for two days? His year is ruined. What happens if B's car breaks down in December and he can't get out there to see customers? What happens if B get the flu in December and he's on his back for two days? Those two bad days equaled one bad year.

And of course you know what happens in January. In January B becomes one of those people that tells you how they could have bought a building 30 years ago for $9. Because what is B telling you? "You know, I could have made my quota. I'm supposed to know it's going to snow? I'm supposed to know the cars going to break down? I'm supposed to know I'm going to get the flu?" Well of course, snow, Chicago, December, what's the chance? One-to-one?

Actually he is right. He's not supposed to know that. But you know what he is supposed to know? That something is going to happen. How do we know that something is going to happen? It always does.

Let me make a brash predication here. Tomorrow when you come into your office, you're going to get interrupted. I guarantee it. I just see this in my mind. I'm predicting this now like the amazing Kreskin.

Somehow I think tomorrow your manager or boss is going to approach you with a crisis that will have to be handled immediately. What's the chances of that? One-to-two. You see we know every day that tomorrow something's going to happen. We don't know what it is, but we know it's there.

So why do we always set ourselves up to let that one bad day give us one bad quarter, one bad month or one bad year? See A, she knew that. She realized that she was in control. She realized the time to worry about December was not in December. The time to worry about December was right here in January and February.

That's what happens when you have a plan. That's what happens when you break it down into continuous action, accomplishable steps, and give yourself the ability to measure your progress every step of the way. That puts you always in control.

Exercise

Now you know that the plan should be expressed in continuous action, accomplishable steps and give you the ability to measure your progress every step of the way. Here is the way to document your plan. Take three blank sheets of paper.

- At the very top of that first blank sheet of paper, write out whatever you designated as goal number one. Write out the first goal in full at the top of that page along with the year you intend to achieve it by.

- Turn to the second page. Do the same thing with your goal number two. Write out the goal in full at the top of the page, along with the year you intend to achieve it by.

- Do the same thing with goal number three on the third page. Write it out in full at the top of the page along with the year you intend to achieve it by.

- Now you have three separate sheets of paper with a goal written across the top of each page along with your timeframe or your year you want to achieve it by.

Next, go back to your first goal. I want you to remember this, you cannot *do* a goal. You can only *work toward* a goal. List the steps you will take to achieve each one of these three goals. Do it now. Remember what I talked about. See yourself successful. As you're writing down the steps that you will take to achieve each one of these three goals, try to visualize yourself actually doing it.

Now, you have a plan. You have a road map. Do you know how long it took you to do that? That's right. You set goals and formulated a plan for three of those goals for the next five years. It took you fourteen minutes. Most people don't do it.

You have a plan. You have the beginnings of a five-year plan. You've finished the third step.

1. Step One: We've seen ourselves successful, visualized it, created a picture in our mind, focused on the picture, and described it to its most minute detail.

2. Step Two: We wrote it down. We wrote down the goal. We set the goal. We put a time frame on it.

3. Step Three: We decided what steps we would have to take to achieve the goal. We planned it out.

That is something very valuable. You have something that will work for you, if you make it work. You have a set of destinations for yourself and some timeframes. You have a road map that will help get you to those destinations that you set for yourself.

Plan It Out—Your Sales Calls

Having a plan for achieving our goals is just as important in our sales career as it is in our lives. And now that you have learned how to do the three steps, let's look at how to use these skills even more, by writing down our goals for a meeting with a customer, or a prospect. This is absolutely critical. You should be planning out every single sales call, every single meeting you have with a customer or a prospect. You should be doing this, at minimum, the day before. Why the day before? The simplest reason is that so many of us have all of these great intentions. I'm going to get to work very early the next morning. I'll come in extra early. Plan out my day, plan out my agenda for this meeting with the prospect, and then I'll get rolling.

And you know what happens? Those streets of the world are paved with the greatest of intentions and we get in the next morning, and what happens? Boom. Crisis hits. And, the next thing we know, is we're planning our agenda as we're in the customer's parking lot.

So, always plan the night before. Use your planning time as the last act you do of the day. You always plan the next day as your last act you did of the previous day. And, it's good to write it down, because you're focusing on exactly what you want to say. It stops you from doing a lot of unnecessary talking that many salespeople do. It focuses more clearly.

It helps to keep that sales call short, especially on a business-to-business call. That's important, because the prospect, or a customer, doesn't have a lot of time. If you're dealing with business people, they don't have a lot of time. They don't want to sit around and hear two-hour sales presentations. They want you in. They want you out. They want to know, "What is this going to do for me? "Show me now what it's going to do for me, how is this going to fill my needs, and get out of here."

When we're on the phone, we have very little time to find out what our prospect wants. Therefore, preplanning is critical to a successful phone presentation. Here are the **THREE** things I would recommend for creating your scripts.

Before you pick up the phone, always ask yourself, what is the purpose of this call? There could be a number of purposes for a call.

- The purpose of a call could be actually making a sales presentation and closing the sale over the phone.

- The purpose of your call could be making a brief presentation and qualifying that prospect as to whether they could be a qualified prospect or customer for your products or services.

- You could be making a call that is geared towards getting you in the door, making a call to get an appointment.

- Number One: If you're making a call to close a sale, then you have to prepare a presentation over the phone, much in the same way as you prepare a presentation to go in person.

- Number Two: As for a qualifying call, you want to prepare the type of telephone script that tells them about your services, asks them if they ever use those kind of services, how they've used those kind of services.

- Number Three: If you are making a call to get an appointment, use the kind of telephone script and preplanning that's geared towards selling one thing and one thing only. The time you're coming over, because why sell on the phone if you're going to get to go there in person?

*   *   *

Preplanning sales is a valuable tool for giving us direction for our actions. We gain the courage to act, not react, to whatever the sales situation brings up.

Our sales preplanning process can also help us anticipate where we might walk away from a customer without trying to get the sale. There has to be a point in your preplanning process where you ask yourself at what point am I willing to walk away from this sale because it doesn't look like it's going to be a good one? I think you have to always take that into consideration. The key to good negotiating is knowing there is some point where you're willing to walk away from the table. That is the only way you're going to come out on top in a negotiation. If you're not willing to walk away from the table, then that tells me you're willing to accept any terms, whether they are good ones or bad ones.

You have to be strong enough and confident enough to know there is a point in any negotiation where you must say, I will not go below this price, or I will not go below these standards, and you must stick to it.

This is hard to do it, for most salespeople, and often because many don't talk to or see enough people, so they feel they have to take whatever they can get. The salesperson who is always prospecting, who is out there seeing more people than anybody else, doesn't have to deal with people that take advantage of them. They can walk away from those people because they have a lot of other people to see. If you have no one else to see, you've got to take whatever's thrown at you. If you have plenty of other people to see, you don't have to take the crummy sales.

This is why I don't like to tell new salespeople to qualify. Everybody's hooked on qualifying calls, make sure everybody's qualified. To my thinking, qualifying is very overrated. You know when you should qualify? When you can come to me, open up your weekly calendar and say, "I can't possibly fit another appointment into my week."

Then, I will tell you to qualify. But, if you have nobody else to see, do me a favor, and just go. Don't qualify. Because, even if they're not qualified, I'll guarantee they know three other people who are.

Act On It

Step five is where the successful people will really start to separate themselves from everybody else. Because while you've seen it, visualized it, created a picture, focused, described, set your goals and planned it out, step four simply says, You have to act. You have to start. You have to do something. You know why? You have twenty-four hours to act on a good idea.

If you do absolutely nothing about a good idea within twenty-four hours, that good idea is dead. Over the course of reading this eBook, hopefully, I have thrown many good ideas at you. I make you a personal guarantee and that is this: If you take all of these good ideas and throw them in a drawer and do absolutely nothing with them, my personal guarantee to you is this: they won't work.

I'm not saying you have to do everything within 24 hours. But what you have to do within 24 hours is to take at least one action step. You've got to do something. Why? Because that's the only way you're going to keep the enthusiasm going.

Did you ever have a good idea? When do you get the most excited about your good ideas? When you first get them. If you don't do something about it right away the enthusiasm starts to waiver. A week later, it's not as high as it was a week ago. Two weeks later it's not as high as it was a week ago.

If you don't do something, any little, tiny action step, every single day, you don't keep that enthusiasm going. You want to make this plan work? You've got to work it.

Those of you that are used to setting goals, what you might want to do, is go beyond the three you set. Take the rest of the goals that you set, do the same thing. Put each one on a separate piece of paper; list the steps you'll take to achieve those goals.

Those of you that aren't comfortable doing that, don't. Just stay with the three. Remember, slow changes folks. I just want you to do what's comfortable for you. I just don't want you to go beyond what's comfortable for you, because I don't want you to get frustrated. I just want you to do a little bit more than you used to. So, stay with the three.

But take the goals you set. Take the plans you've made, and post them up somewhere where you can see them every single day. If you see them every single day, you're going to move toward them every single day.

That old expression may sound simple but it rings true, out of sight, out of mind. If you see that goal, if you see that plan up on the wall every single day, you're going to remember it. You're going to want it more every single day. You're going to move toward it every single day, and if you're not moving toward it and you're looking at it every day, you're going to have to answer to that one person you can't fool, you.

We will always move toward our most dominant thoughts. Why don't we make what we want out of our lives our most dominant thoughts? If we put them up somewhere, where we can see them every day, we'll move toward them every day.

Along with seeing it every day, remember to keep reviewing it on a consistent basis. Look at it, at least every six months. Why? Your life changes. Your priorities change. Maybe a goal for you today, might not seem that important six months from now. You might not really care about it. It's okay. Cross it off. Get rid of it. It's all right. It's yours. This is your plan.

Let's keep in mind that you used a pen or a pencil and paper, not a hammer and chisel and a block of stone. It's all yours. If you don't want it anymore, get rid of the goal. If it's not important, get rid of it. If you've achieved all of you goals, what do you do? Set some more. Yes, it's yours.

What happens if you get to your deadline and you haven't achieved the goal yet? Move back the deadline. That's the beauty of your plan. It's yours. Do not be those people who think that if they get to the deadline and they haven't achieved the goal, they've failed.

Remember there are no goal setting police who will come to your house, it doesn't happen. You set a new goal. It's yours. You do whatever you want with it. But, it will only work to the degree that you make it work.

The most important piece is that you've got to start. You've got to act. You've got to do something. Most people talk about all of the great things they're going to do with their lives. That's all they ever do.

A friend of mine has been telling me he's going to start his own business for many years. I always ask what kind of business. He says, "I'm going to go into the mail order business." And he wants to go into the mail order business because he's one of those people who figures that it's easy. All you've got to do is mail stuff out and you sit and people send you money. And, every time I see him I ask, "How come you haven't started your business yet?" And, he says, "It's okay I will, I'm gathering information."

Finally, after nine years of this, I said to him, you know you're wrong. You shouldn't go into the mail order business. You should open a library. You certainly have enough information. Do you think he's ever going to do it? He'll talk about it. He'll rationalize it, but he won't write it down, because if he writes it down, he's got to admit he's not doing it.

You've got to act. You've got to start. You've got to do something.

Acting on our goals is a most critical part of the entire process of achieving our best. And, acting on our goals is not a one-time affair. I want to stress the importance of doing something every day to further our goals.

And I do mean every single day. What I don't mean, is that you have to do something big every single day. What I mean is, do *something*. Even if it's the tiniest, smallest, action step. Just try to get in the habit of doing something every single day.

By doing something small you maintain the habit, and by maintaining the habit, you maintain the enthusiasm. Let me give you an example.

A very good friend of mine decided about seven or eight months ago that he needed to get in shape. He had never exercised; he just felt he really wanted to work on getting and staying in shape. He decided that he wanted to create the habit of exercise in his life and that the only way to do it was to spend a full year working out every single day.

He does not go to a gym and run ten miles and work out on weight machines every single day. He does make sure that at least once a day he does some sort of exercise, and he does travel a lot. He told me if he hasn't done anything that day, even if it's eleven fifty-seven at night, he'll get down on the floor and do ten sit ups.

That is not what we would call a heavy duty workout, but do you see what it is he's done? He has maintained the habit, just by that little action. That tiny action of the ten sit ups, lets him say to himself, "I exercised today." And when he says, "I exercised today," he says it with such enthusiasm because he takes great accomplishment in the fact that he did it again. He spent another day doing what he set out to do. And he's so enthusiastic about it, that there's no way he's not going to do it tomorrow.

It is not a matter of doing something big every day, it is about doing something no matter how small. Just do something.

It is important to know you are able to adjust your target, to change the date of your goal. I want to address how this is different from that other bad habit we discussed: procrastination.

I don't see procrastination is really a factor here. A lot of people think that if you don't get to your goal by the assigned date, by the assigned deadline, that you've failed. But of course you haven't failed. You haven't failed if you haven't given up. If you get to the assigned date and you haven't achieved the goal, remember, it's your goal. It's your date. Move it back and keep going after it.

I don't consider moving back the deadline procrastination. If you're really setting goals and planning in the proper way, you're not taking that goal down. You still have it written. You still have it posted up where you can see it. You've just moved back the deadline. That's all. As long as you keep it up there, keep it visual, as long as you maintain the accountability, it's still a goal. If you haven't reached it by the deadline, readjust the deadline.

I have set goals that I haven't reached that deadline for two or three years in a row. Now, I'm finally starting to accomplish them. That's not procrastination because I never gave up on the goal. Maybe the timing wasn't right. Maybe other things took precedence over that goal. And, because I have my list of goals up there, I was achieving other goals. That wasn't procrastinating. I just didn't happen to get that one done *yet*.

You know when it's procrastination, because you take that goal off of the board. You stick it in the drawer somewhere, sight unseen, never look at it again, and keep saying to yourself, "I should have done that and someday I'll do that. Sometime I'll do that." That's procrastination. As long as you keep the goal written, keep the goal posted up and you keep setting deadlines and timeframes, that goal is real and, eventually, you will achieve it.

The Finale—Your Ideas— Write Them Down!

Just as we need to write down our goals to remind ourselves to act on them, we also need to write down our ideas. How else will we be able to remember them?

Have you ever, in your entire life, have had at least one good idea? Did you ever have one of those ideas where you've think, that would make a good book? Or, a great movie? Or, with a friend say, "You know, this product could be incredible? If we ever got together, put some money behind it and market it right, we could make millions."

And then, a year later, what happens? Somebody else did it. You saw it somewhere else. And you saw it somewhere else, you said, "Hey, that was my idea." So what?

We have seen that everybody has good ideas. Everybody walking the earth has had at least one good idea. But what is the difference? What is the difference is between a good idea and a successful idea? The difference is that they did it. They acted. They did something.

By now you know what my philosophy is that there is no such thing as a bad idea. I really believe that. To me, the only bad ideas are first, the ones that are not acted upon, and second, the ones that are not acted upon properly.

And if you don't believe that there's no such thing as a bad idea, let me give you these four words. Teenage Mutant Ninja Turtles. Did you ever hear of a dumber idea than Teenage Mutant Ninja Turtles? That sounds like one of the dumbest idea in the world.

Let me remind you about them. These are little green crime-fighting turtles. They live in the sewer. Their boss is a rat. And, they eat nothing but pizza. It is the dumbest idea in the world. But they are a franchise spanning movies, videogames, cartoons, toys, games, books, comic books, clothing. They have grossed over three billion dollars with considerable worldwide success and fame, and it is the dumbest idea in the world.

What if somebody had come to you and said, "I've got the greatest idea in the world. I'm going to make you rich beyond your wildest imagination. Give me a check. I'll make you a partner. Wait until you hear what it is. Here it is. Ready? Teenage Mutant Ninja Turtles!"

"I know what you're thinking. But let me tell you what they are. These are little, green crime-fighting turtles. They live in the sewer. Their boss is a rat. And they eat nothing but pizza. Are you in?" You might have said, "Are you crazy?"

You know who else said that? Hasbro. The number one toy maker in the world. They said, "No one will ever buy little green turtles that live in the sewer."

That's why I've said to you and will repeat it one final time: **There is no such thing as a bad idea. But you have to start. You have to act. You've got to do something.**